WATER FUN
and Fitness

Terri Elder
Wichita State University

Human Kinetics

ing-in-Publication Data

1. Aquatic exercises.   2. Water--Recreational use.   3. Aquatic
sports--Safety measures.   I. Title.
GV838.53.E94E44   1995
613.7'16--dc20
                                                      95-2204
                                                        CIP

ISBN: 0-87322-501-5

Acquisitions Editor: Richard D. Frey, PhD; **Developmental Editors:** Ann Brodsky, Mary E. Fowler, and Larret Galasyn-Wright; **Assistant Editor:** Julie Marx Ohnemus **Copyeditor:** Nedra Lambert; **Proofreader:** Karin Leszczynski; **Typesetter:** Francine Hamerski; **Text Designer:** Judy Henderson; **Layout Artist:** Tara Welsch; **Cover Designer:** Jack Davis; **Cover Photographer:** © Jeff Greenberg/Unicorn Stock Photos; **Illustrators:** Bruce Morton and Tom Janowski; **Printer:** United Graphics

Human Kinetics books are available at special discounts for bulk purchase. Special editions or book excerpts can also be created to specification. For details, contact the Special Sales Manager at Human Kinetics.

Printed in the United States of America   10 9 8 7 6 5 4 3 2 1

Human Kinetics
P.O. Box 5076, Champaign, IL 61825-5076
1-800-747-4457

Canada: Human Kinetics, Box 24040,
Windsor, ON N8Y 4Y9
1-800-465-7301 (in Canada only)

Europe: Human Kinetics,
P.O. Box IW14, Leeds LS16 6TR, United Kingdom
(44) 1132 781708

Australia: Human Kinetics, 2 Ingrid Street,
Clapham 5062, South Australia
(08) 371 3755

New Zealand: Human Kinetics, P.O. Box 105-231, Auckland 1
(09) 523 3462

To the students at Newton High School who participated in the freshman swimming classes during my 12 years of tenure, and to a very special group of kids in the special education program who put up with my antics. Thank you to Jackie, Kelly, Gilbert, Sharyl, Catherine, Elizabeth, Kevin, Julian, Penny, Sabrina, and Susan for teaching me all about water fun. The memories that we shared will be forever in my heart. Thanks to Deb (Hefley) Collier for her love and support and to Jan Hoberecht for reviewing the first draft of this manuscript.

Contents

Activity Finder   vii
Preface   xvii
Credits   xix

Chapter 1   Introduction   1

Selecting Activities   2
Adapting Games and Stunts for Individual Needs   4
Using Equipment to Enhance Play and Learning   5
Attending to Risk Management   5
Ensuring Personal Safety   9

Chapter 2   Stunts and Skills   15

Individual Activities   16
Partner Activities   39
Group Activities   52

Chapter 3   Games   63

Relays   63
Heads-Up Activities   71
Swimming Activities   84

Chapter 4   Fitness Activities   91

Water Exercise   92
Leg Works   94
Arm Works   102
Fun and Funky Choreography   109
Water Circuit   115
Swimming   116

Appendix A   Skills Assessment Grid   124

Appendix B   Equipment for Water Fun and Safety   125

Appendix C   Aquatic Equipment Resource List   127

Appendix D   Cooper 12-Minute Swimming Test   128

Appendix E   The Ball State 500-Yard Water Run Test   129

About the Author   131

Activity Finder

The Activity Finder is arranged so that, at a glance, you can find the appropriate game/activity based on the skill levels within your group. The activities are classified as individual, mixed pairs, partners, mixed group, group, aquatic exercise, or fitness swimming. The word *mixed* in these headings refers to activities in which one person (in the mixed pair) or more than one person (in the mixed group) is not a swimmer and will not be required to submerge during the activity.

Prerequisite skills are provided to help you measure the difficulty of the activity. These prerequisites include independent locomotion, breath control, submersion, underwater swimming, floating, and swimming skills. For the purposes of this book, we'll use the following definitions.

Independent locomotion is, at minimum, the ability to remain upright in chest-deep water and walk comfortably around the playing area without having to hang on to the side of the pool.

Breath control refers to air exchanging and breath holding. Participants should be able to hold their breath for a minimum of 3 seconds.

Submersion means being able to completely submerge and hold breath for a minimum of 5 seconds.

Underwater swimming refers to the ability to submerge at least 3 feet underwater and make some forward progress while maintaining a horizontal position.

Floating (front or back) means staying on the surface of the water without support. It is not necessary for participants to remain in a horizontal position while floating.

Swimming skill refers to horizontal (feet off the bottom) locomotion. However, standard swimming strokes are not often required, and participants may swim with the face up in any manner they choose.

Some of the activity descriptions list other skill prerequisites that can be used as lead-up activities. These are not listed in the Activity Finder. Other pertinent information includes water depth, need for equipment, and whether variations exist for the activity. Many of the activities have one or more deep-water variations. To ensure safety for the deep-water variations, be sure that all participants can swim at least two lengths of the pool comfortably using any stroke and are able to tread water for a minimum of 2 minutes in deep water.

Key

Activity type

I = Individual

MP = Mixed pairs*

P = Partners

MG = Mixed group*

G = Group

AqX = Aquatic exercise

FS = Fitness swimming

* Mixed pairs and mixed groups indicate that one person (in a pair) or more than one person (in a group) are nonswimmers and will not submerge during the activity.

Prerequisite skills

L = Independent locomotion

BC = Breath control

S = Submersion

US = Underwater swimming

F = Floating

Sw = Swimming skills

Activity Finder

Name of the activity	Page	Activity type	Prerequi-site skills	Water depth	Equipment	Variations
Aqua Man Relay	69	G	S BC US	Shallow	No	No
Back Dolphin	37	I	S BC Sw	Deep	No	No
Back Tuck Somersault	37	I	S BC Sw	Deep	No	No
Ball Relay	68	G	Sw	Shallow	Yes	Yes
Balloon Relay	67	G	Sw	Shallow	Yes	Yes
Baseball	87	MG	L Sw	All depths	Yes	Yes
Beach Ball Volleyball	81	MG	L	Shallow	Yes	Yes
Big Splash Contest	89	G	Sw	Deep	Yes	Yes
Blowing a Floating Object	19	I	L	Shallow	Yes	Yes
Buddy Bobs	43	P	L S BC	Shallow	No	Yes
Buddy Swim Relay	65	G	S BC Sw	Shallow	No	Yes
Buddy Swims	47	P	S BC Sw	All depths	No	No
Bunny Hop	109	MG AqX	L	Shallow	No	Yes

Activity Finder

Name of the activity	Page	Activity type	Prerequisite skills	Water depth	Equipment	Variations
Catch-Up Swims	117	G FS	Sw	All depths	No	Yes
Chain Dolphin	50	P	S BC Sw	Deep	No	No
Circles Around the Pool	119	G FS	Sw	All depths	No	Yes
Circles in the Lane	120	G FS	Sw	All depths	No	No
Corkscrew Swims	32	I	S BC Sw	Shallow	No	Yes
Crack the Whip	53	MG	L	Shallow	No	Yes
Crisscross	119	G FS	Sw	All depths	No	No
Dare Base	78	MG	L	Shallow	No	Yes
Down the River	59	G	L F	Shallow	No	No
Fill a Hole	80	MG	L	Shallow	No	Yes
Fire Pole	23	I	S BC	Shallow	Yes	Yes
Fish Flop	22	I	L	Shallow	No	No
Flag Tag	76	MG	L	Shallow	Yes	Yes

Activity Finder

Name of the activity	Page	Activity type	Prerequisite skills	Water depth	Equipment	Variations
Flip-Flops	27	I	L	Shallow	Yes	Yes
Float Patterns	61	MG	L	Shallow	No	Yes
Follow the Leader	84	G	S BC Sw	Shallow	No	Yes
Four Corners	118	G FS	Sw	All depths	No	Yes
Front Somersault	37	I	S BC Sw	Deep	No	No
Funky Steps	112	MG AqX	L	Shallow	No	Yes
Fusion Tag	77	MG	L	Shallow	No	No
Gutter Laps	118	MG FS	L	NA	No	No
Gutter Walk	16	I	None	NA	No	Yes
Human Cork	24	I	S BC	Shallow	No	No
Human Croquet	45	P	S BC US	Shallow	No	No
Human Croquet Relay	70	G	S BC US	Shallow	No	Yes
Humming	20	I	None	Shallow	No	Yes

Activity Finder

Name of the activity	Page	Activity type	Prerequisite skills	Water depth	Equipment	Variations
Independent Kicking	19	I	L	Shallow	Yes	Yes
Independent Locomotion	17	I	None	Shallow	No	No
Jets	21	I	L	Shallow	No	Yes
Kickboard Stunts	28	I	L S BC	Shallow	Yes	Yes
Kip	36	I	S BC Sw	Deep	No	No
Leapfrog	44	P	L S BC	Shallow	No	Yes
Life Jacket Water Polo	82	MG	Sw	Deep	Yes	Yes
Listening Underwater	21	I	S BC	Shallow	Yes	No
Log Rolls	31	I	L S BC F	Shallow	No	No
Lying on the Bottom	26	I	S BC	Shallow	No	No
Medley Dash	64	MG	Sw	Shallow	No	Yes
Mini Triathlon/ Biathlon	122	MG FS	L	Shallow	No	Yes
Musical Kickboards	75	MG	L	Shallow	Yes	Yes

Activity Finder

Name of the activity	Page	Activity type	Prerequi- site skills	Water depth	Equipment	Variations
Object Retrieval	24	I	L S BC	Shallow	Yes	Yes
Object Retrieval Race	72	MG	L	Shallow	Yes	Yes
Old Faithful	18	I	L	Shallow	No	No
Old MacDonald	56	G	L S BC	Shallow	No	Yes
Over and Under	58	MG	L	Shallow	Yes	No
Over and Under Relay	71	MG	L	Shallow	Yes	Yes
Oyster	38	I	S BC Sw	Deep	No	No
Partner Flip-Flops	43	MP	L	Shallow	No	No
Partner Hand- stands	46	P	L S BC	Shallow	No	No
Partner Towing	39	MP	L	Shallow	No	Yes
Pass the Splash	56	MG	L	Shallow	No	No
Pigeon Race	73	MG	L	Shallow	No	Yes
Pike Surface Dive	36	I	S BC Sw	Deep	No	No

Activity Finder

Name of the activity	Page	Activity type	Prerequisite skills	Water depth	Equipment	Variations
Pinball Tag	78	MG	L	Shallow	No	Yes
Planking	49	P	S BC F	Shallow	No	No
Porpoise Dives	28	I	L S BC	Shallow	No	No
Push Me War	42	MP	L	Shallow	No	Yes
Rag Tag	85	G	L S	All depths	Yes	Yes
Red Light, Green Light	74	MG	L	Shallow	No	Yes
Sculling	33	I	F	All depths	No	Yes
Sitting on the Bottom	25	I	S BC	Shallow	No	No
Sky Ball	52	MG	L	Shallow	Yes	Yes
Sock and Shirt Relay	66	G	Sw	Shallow	Yes	Yes
Splash the Teacher	52	MG	L	Shallow	No	No
Square Dance Moves	109	MG AqX	L	Shallow	No	Yes
Squid Swim	30	I	L S BC	Shallow	No	No

Activity Finder

Name of the activity	Page	Activity type	Prerequi-site skills	Water depth	Equipment	Variations
Stuff It	60	MG	L	Shallow	Yes	No
Stunt Circle	54	MG	L	Shallow	No	Yes
Swim the English Channel	121	MG FS	L Sw	All depths	No	Yes
Swim the Waves	87	G	L Sw	Shallow	Yes	Yes
Tangle	86	G	L S	Shallow	No	No
Thread the Needle	51	P	L S BC	Shallow	No	No
Tidal Wave	17	MG	None	NA	No	No
Tug-of-War	79	MG	L	Shallow	Yes	Yes
Underdog Tag	85	G	S BC US	Shallow	No	Yes
Under-water Hockey	88	G	L S BC US	Shallow	Yes	Yes
Washing Machine	57	G	L S BC F	Shallow	No	Yes
Water Bucket	55	MG	L	Shallow	No	No
Water Circuit	115	MG AqX	L	Shallow	Yes	Yes

Activity Finder

Name of the activity	Page	Activity type	Prerequi- site skills	Water depth	Equipment	Variations
Water Exercise	92	MG AqX	L	Shallow	No	Yes
Water Gymnastics	32	I	S BC	Shallow	No	Yes
Wheel- barrow	40	MP	L	Shallow	No	Yes
Wheelies	41	MP	L	Shallow	No	Yes
Whistle Stop Stunt Race	84	G	L S BC	Shallow	No	Yes
Zigzags	117	G FS	Sw	All depths	No	Yes

Preface

Structured aquatic programs for children and youth are extremely popular in the United States. Most programs organize participants with similar skills into small groups to enhance skill acquisition. Unfortunately, many physical educators, program specialists, and youth activities coordinators do not have this option. They are burdened with the task of providing safe aquatic experiences for large groups in which skill levels may vary from apprehensive beginners to competitive swimmers. This dilemma often discourages supervisors and educators from including structured water play in their programs and classes.

Water Fun and Fitness was written as a resource to address the special needs of aquatic specialists, recreation professionals, youth agency personnel, and elementary, middle school, and secondary physical educators who must work with large, integrated groups of individuals in an aquatic setting. It is written for children and youth ages K through 12 and contains a reader-friendly collection of stunts, skills, games, and fitness ideas that are designed to make learning safe, exciting, and fun. To assist you in preparing your individuals for more challenging games and activities, basic water adjustment and stroke readiness skills are included as well.

Chapter 1 of *Water Fun and Fitness* addresses how to evaluate the skills of your group and adapt activities for individual needs, and ends with information relating to the safe management of your aquatic recreation activities. Chapter 2 is devoted to stunts and skills that are non-competitive in nature. Some of these activities require the participants to go underwater, but many are designed to prepare them for the underwater experience and to make them more comfortable being in the water.

Chapter 3 builds on the stunts and skills in chapter 2. Many of the relays and games described in chapter 3 use the activities in the previous chapter to increase the challenge and competitive nature of the aquatic experience. Chapter 3 includes a section of games that do not require the participants to go underwater and a section to challenge better swimmers. Chapter 4 covers water fitness activities. Some activities, such as water fitness performed in a vertical position, do not require swimming skills. There are also more challenging fitness activities for participants who are comfortable with the swimming skills.

The majority of the activities presented in this book can be conducted in shallow water and require very little, if any, swimming skill. Better swimmers will find the deep-water variations and partner stunts and skills novel and challenging. Many of these activities have been used with developmentally disabled youth and adults. It is not necessary for those who conduct the activities in *Water Fun and Fitness* to possess exceptional swimming skill. They only need to have a true interest in providing a safe aquatic learning experience and a desire to help children and youth become comfortable in the water and have waves of fun doing it.

Credits

The Facility Safety Checklist on page 7 is adapted from *Aquatic Fitness Everyone* (p. 290), by T. Elder and K. Campbell, 1993, Winston-Salem, NC: Hunter Textbooks. Copyright 1993 by Hunter Textbooks, Inc. Adapted by permission.

Appendix D is adapted from "1.5 Mile Tests" from *The Aerobics Program for Total Well Being* by Kenneth H. Cooper, M.D., M.P.H. Copyright © 1982 by Kenneth H. Cooper. Used by permission of Bantam Books, a division of Bantam Doubleday Dell Publishing Group, Inc.

Appendix E is reprinted from "The Ball State 500-Yard Water Run: A New Fitness Field Test for Non-Swimming Water Exercisers," by G. Robbins and D. Powers, 1993, *Journal of the International Council for Health, Physical Education, Recreation, Sport, and Dance*, **29**, p. 11, by permission of the International Council for Health, Physical Education, Recreation, Sport, and Dance.

Introduction

The water is an exciting, inviting medium for activity. It has a natural beauty that lures children into participation. This chapter will help you find ways to make water learning fun, enjoyable, and safe. You'll discover how to find fun in activities that do not require submersion. And you won't feel compelled to teach swimming skills. You'll find that the game approach will enhance the water learning, and children will not even realize that they are learning skills through play.

As you read chapters 2 through 4 of this book—"Stunts and Skills," "Games," and "Fitness Activities"—you'll find an introduction to each chapter that gives a brief rationale for including the skills in your program or class. The activities in each chapter are arranged from easiest to most challenging. This creates a natural progression of skills and encourages more success along the way. It is important for you to prepare a lesson plan for each class, define objectives, and select appropriate activities to meet the objectives of each lesson. For safety purposes, do not engage in spur-of-the-moment activities, as unplanned activities may lead to potentially dangerous situations.

Your teaching methods should be consistent with the latest information on teaching aquatics to young people. If you decide to adapt a game or skill from this book, be sure that you take a safe, conservative approach. Discuss all safety information about the activity with the students and document it in the lesson plan.

Selecting Activities

Select activities that are age and skill appropriate. The younger the child, the less complex the game should be. Be sure that youngsters possess the prerequisite skills necessary to successfully participate in the game, stunt, or skill. Do not overload the activity time with games for competition. Be sure to provide a mix of individual and group experiences.

Provide some form of skill assessment (such as the stunt circle described next) before you begin your activity class or program. It is not unusual to have good swimmers and nonswimmers in the same group. You should know your class well before you teach aquatic activities. See Appendix A for a sample skills assessment checklist.

Stunt Circle

The *stunt circle* is a quick, safe, nonthreatening approach to assessing the water adjustment and swimming skills of your group. No swimming skills are necessary, and participants do not have to get their faces wet to participate unless and until they want to or are ready to.

Organize the group into one large circle in standing-depth water (chest deep, if possible). Have participants count off by twos. If the number in the circle is uneven, you will need to join the circle during the assessment. If the number is even, stand outside the circle and give directions. To set up the circle for assessment, have the ones support the twos. Ones keep their feet on the bottom of the pool using a wide base of support (feet shoulder-width apart and knees bent slightly). They support by reaching under the arms and across the backs of the twos on either side of them. The assessment begins with the twos doing supported front and back floats in the circle. Give directions using a movement exploration format: "Who can do (*selected movement*)?"

Have the group attempt the following skills:

- Front float with face out of the water (feet should be on the surface outside the circle)
- Front float, face out, and flutter kick
- Nose bubbles with eyes above the surface
- Front float, face in, to the count of three, four, or five
- Front float, face in, and kick
- Back float with feet on the surface (participants will have feet on the inside of the circle)
- Back float and kick
- Back float with ears wet
- Back float, ears wet, and kick

Make a mental note of students who seem apprehensive (those who will not submerge on the front float, those who will not get their ears wet on the back float, and those who continue to move, wiggle, or thrash about even when the skill should be performed motionless). Have the twos support and the ones try the skills. Try the circle again with a new challenge. Instead of supporting with the arms across the back, have the participants hold hands. Challenge the participants to let go of hands during the skills whenever possible. Make a mental note of those who cannot do skills unsupported. Later you can fill in the checklist in Appendix A to help identify students' needs. Use the Activity Finder to select games that are appropriate to the skills of the group as a whole.

Adapting Games and Stunts for Individual Needs

The Americans with Disabilities Act and similar legislation encourage the mainstreaming of individuals with disabilities into regular classes. It is not unlikely that you will have students with special needs in your class or group. Do not assume that all such individuals need special adaptations, especially in the aquatic setting. The buoyancy of the water supports movements and allows many people with noticeable disabilities the freedom to move independently.

Before providing adaptations for your students, give them the opportunity to try the skills involved in the activity. If they are unsuccessful, you will have some idea of their personal abilities and can adjust the game or stunt accordingly. The following information provides you with some options for adapting games to fit your students.

• *Change the rules.*   Younger children need less complex rules to understand and enjoy the games. Make the game simple.

• *Change the size of the area.*   Make the play area smaller for less advanced swimmers. Use the whole pool for more advanced groups.

• *Use a different depth of water or various depths.*   Move a deep-water game to chest deep. Challenge good swimmers by requiring that they play in deep water only. Use all areas of the pool.

• *Have all participants wear a life jacket.*   Be sure that everyone is comfortable in shallow and deep water with the life jacket on and can perform a simple swimming stroke well enough to return to the side of the pool independently. You can use the whole pool area and make the game fun for nonswimmers, yet challenging for better swimmers.

• *Provide a handicap for better swimmers.*   You might have better swimmers wear sweatshirts to slow them down or let them swim with only one arm or propel themselves by kicking only. You can also handicap better swimmers by making them jog instead of swim. Jogging is a much slower way to get from place to place.

- *Pair disabled students with nondisabled students.*   In many of the buddy stunts, disabled swimmers or nonswimmers can be paired with a swimming buddy to perform the skill or participate in a game or relay.

Using Equipment to Enhance Play and Learning

Equipment can add a new dimension to a water activity class. Most pools have certain equipment such as kickboards and buoys available to all users. Other facilities have fins, hand paddles, and other training equipment available as well. If your budget does not allow you to purchase pool play equipment, look in your physical education supplies and see what equipment you can adapt for the pool. Many balls, including golf balls and rubber sport balls, can increase enjoyment at poolside. Wiffle ball equipment can also be used successfully in the pool area. More information about equipment and equipment safety appears in Appendix B. Appendix C provides a resource list for pool and play equipment.

Attending to Risk Management

Safety is a major concern in an aquatic program. Safe water activities require good organization and planning. Instructors are encouraged to teach basic water safety skills as part of the program and to encourage safe play in and around the water.

Risk management is a process of identifying and managing the risks of an activity with the intent of reducing the incidence of injury to the participants. Risk management is a shared responsibility. Facility operators are responsible for facility safety and, in most cases, for the supervision of the patrons. Program supervisors and instructors must plan for safety during the activities and programs they conduct. Although the aquatic environment by its nature will always hold an element of risk, a comprehensive risk management plan can reduce the injury potential of aquatic activities.

Safe Facilities

In most cases, the instructor or supervisor of a program does not have direct responsibility for the operation of the facility. However, a safe program begins with a safe facility. Before the program begins, tour the facility that you intend to use. Find out if lifeguard supervision will be provided for your program. It may be necessary for you to assume that responsibility. Check the facility for safety hazards. Look for clear, sparkling water. Murky water can reduce visibility and hamper supervision. The deck, locker room, and shower areas should have slip-resistant surfaces. There should be no areas where standing water can cause falls. The deck and pool should also be free of obstructions. There should be a safety line that divides the shallow area from the deep, and water depths should be clearly marked on the deck at different areas around the pool.

The facility checklist on the next page provides additional information on the pool safety check. If you find areas of concern, bring them to the attention of the pool operator immediately. You will have to decide if the risks you have identified can be managed with good program/activity safety. If not, you may need to reconsider using this facility.

Safe Programs

As you plan your program, be aware of aquatic activities that increase the chance of personal injury. Plan your program to eliminate or control these activities. The most dangerous activities/situations in a pool area are

- swimming underwater after hyperventilating,
- diving into shallow water,
- horseplay,
- unsupervised use of scuba equipment,
- overcrowding of the pool,
- tag games,
- follow the leader off the springboard, and
- unsupervised use of flotation devices by children.

You can minimize the risks by providing good supervision, establishing and enforcing rules, planning for possible emergencies, and teaching personal safety skills to your group.

Supervision.   The ability to adequately supervise an aquatic activity program depends a great deal on the professional training of the staff and the instructor-to-student ratio. Ideally, there should be a lifeguard supervising the activity. In the absence of a lifeguard, you should be trained in water rescue (preferably trained in lifeguarding, first aid, and CPR), and you must remain on deck (elevated if possible) to ensure

FACILITY SAFETY CHECKLIST

Pool Deck

- ☐ Clean, nonslip surface
- ☐ Free of obstructions
- ☐ Depth markings
- ☐ Air temperature 3° to 5° above pool temperature
- ☐ Adequate lighting

Pool Bottom

- ☐ Smooth, gentle sloping bottom
- ☐ Marked for depth perception

Steps/Ladders

- ☐ Nonslip surfaces
- ☐ Handrails secured properly
- ☐ Steps marked with contrasting color

Pool Water

- ☐ Clear, sparkling water
- ☐ Temperature between 82° and 86°F
- ☐ No strong odor of chlorine

Safety Equipment

- ☐ Long reaching pole
- ☐ Ring buoy or other throwing device
- ☐ Safety line separating shallow from deep end
- ☐ Rules posted
- ☐ Telephone or other communication system
- ☐ First aid equipment, including a backboard
- ☐ Elevated lifeguard stands

Even if your facility seems reasonably safe, it is still important to develop a regular pattern of inspection. Check the facility and equipment daily. Make sure that safety equipment is available and in good condition. Equipment used for class activities should be in good repair. Do not use faulty equipment.

the safety of the class. This means you cannot demonstrate skills or help students who need additional assistance mastering skills.

If a lifeguard is available, the facility size, the area of shallow water available, and the skill level of the group will determine how many students you can safely teach and supervise. One recommended standard suggests that each swimmer should have about 40 square feet of surface area for shallow-water swimming instruction. In *Swimming Pools: A Guide to Their Planning, Design, and Operation*, M. Alexander Gabrielsen suggests that a more advanced group may require only 20 square feet of surface area. There should be at least one lifeguard for each 30 to 50 participants in an organized aquatic activity. Add another lifeguard if the group exceeds 50 participants.

You can improve your chances of maintaining a safe program if you involve the class or group in the safety of the program. Establish a communication system. For example, one short whistle means *everyone freeze*. Two short whistles means *buddy check*. One long whistle means *clear the pool*. Three short whistles means *resume play*. Teach the participants about the *buddy system*. Each person is assigned or may choose a buddy to keep track of during the activity. Each *buddy pair* has a number. On the signal (two short whistles) buddies clasp hands and hold them above their heads. As soon as the group is quiet, the buddy pairs count off, beginning with number one and continuing until all pairs have been counted. Any person who cannot locate her buddy during the class activity or for buddy check should report to the lifeguard or supervisor immediately. Clear the pool and begin a search.

Rules.   Establish and consistently enforce rules of the pool. Your facility may have others that are specific to the design of the pool. You may need to establish additional rules to govern class behavior. Provide a copy of the rules for each participant and take time in the first meeting to discuss the rules and reasons for each rule before entering the water. The following rules are considered standard precautions for aquatic safety:

- No running on the deck.
- No spitting or spouting in the pool.
- No horseplay on the deck.
- No pushing or shoving other swimmers into the pool.
- No diving into shallow water.
- No flotation equipment allowed in deep water (exception: Coast Guard-approved life jackets).

Planning for Emergencies.   Although many facilities have an emergency action plan (EAP) to handle a variety of emergencies, it is prudent to prepare your class for such a situation. Be certain that your students understand their role in the emergency procedure. Discuss the emergency signal with the class (one long whistle means *clear the pool*). Select a few responsible individuals to learn how to activate the emergency medical services (EMS) system at your facility. Practice evacuating the pool (much the same as during a fire drill) so that everyone knows where to go. Evacuation of the pool must be organized to avoid complicating rescue efforts. Discuss locker room behavior if the class must evacuate to the locker room while you manage the emergency. If an emergency action plan has not been designed for your facility, you should take the responsibility to do it. Follow these steps when developing an emergency action plan:

- Establish a chain of command.
- Review state and local ordinances.
- Define the potentially dangerous situations for your program.
- Check the availability and condition of existing rescue equipment.
- Locate emergency exits.
- Identify emergency support personnel.
- Display emergency numbers (including ambulance/rescue squad, fire department, physician, electrical company).
- Meet with emergency personnel to discuss procedures.
- Develop the emergency procedures to include provisions for

    — safe rescue,
    — activating the EMS system,
    — continued patron supervision,
    — crowd/traffic control, and
    — notification of the chain of command.

- Rehearse all procedures with support/supervisory staff.

Ensuring Personal Safety

Learning personal safety skills as part of a water activities class will help increase the students' independence in the water. Personal safety skills also provide a progression for stroke and stunt learning. Students who master these skills will be more relaxed in the water and will enjoy a variety of games and stunts.

Independent Entry and Exit

Students should learn how to enter and exit the water independently and in a safe manner. Depending on your facility, this may mean walking down a ramp or sitting on the poolside and sliding into the water. Ladders should be used for exit only. Descending a ladder into the pool is not the safest approach. Teach students to use a jump entry into chest-deep water and to regain a balanced position. Jumping into deep water will require more advanced swimming skills.

Note that better swimmers enjoy using a headfirst or diving entry. Diving into shallow water is a leading cause of spinal injury (in particular, broken necks). Do not allow students to dive into water shallower than 9 feet. Do not teach diving if you have not received proper training in teaching diving progressions.

Breath Control

Breath control involves the ability to hold the breath as well as exchange air through the mouth and nose in a rhythmic manner. Swimming strokes do not require long periods of breath holding, but participants should be comfortable holding their breath for 3 to 5 seconds to enjoy underwater activities. Rhythmic air exchange refers to inhaling through the mouth and exhaling underwater through the mouth and nose. Exhaling through the nose should be emphasized in the early stages of learning to decrease the chances of a person inhaling water up the nose.

Students can learn to exhale through the nose by practicing humming. Humming forces the air out the nose and prevents water from entering. Begin with the chin on the surface of the water. Take a breath, close the lips, and begin humming. Slowly lower the face until the nostrils are just under the surface of the water. The eyes are still out of the water. Humming with the nose submerged makes *nose bubbles*. Another approach is to pretend to *blow your nose* underwater.

Hyperventilation.   Activities that involve extended periods of breath holding can be extremely dangerous. Students may hyperventilate (take a series of long, deep breaths) to extend breath-holding time. This could result in blowing off too much carbon dioxide (CO_2), which triggers the breathing response. Without CO_2 to the brain, the swimmer will not feel the urge to breathe before he runs out of air. Consequently he will black out. If the blackout happens underwater, the swimmer will inhale water and drown.

To avoid the consequences of hyperventilation, discuss the dangers with your group and be watchful during underwater activities. Do not allow participants to take more than two or three long, deep breaths before submerging. Do not encourage breath-holding contests.

Opening Eyes Underwater

Seeing underwater is a unique and exciting experience. At first the eyes might sting a bit, but swimmers will quickly adjust and have little trouble locating objects or other swimmers. Seeing underwater reduces the chance of collisions with other swimmers or with the side of the pool. It also provides swimmers with important kinesthetic feedback about where their bodies are during an activity.

Students who are apprehensive about facial submersion can use goggles to reduce that fear. Goggles actually improve vision. Objects appear 25% closer and 25% larger underwater. Goggles are also appropriate for individuals who wear contacts. If participants will spend the majority of the activity time with eyes open underwater, they should be encouraged to wear goggles to reduce eye irritation. For more information on using goggles, refer to Appendix B.

Unsupported Floating or Gliding

Unsupported floating or gliding is a true step toward independent swimming. Once participants can relax on their front or back and use the water for support, they will begin to experience success in swimming strokes. The prone float or glide requires face-down breath holding. Extend the arms over the head, put the face in the water, and slowly lift the feet off the pool bottom to float (push with the feet to glide forward).

The back float should be started in chest-deep water with the arms extended horizontally to the side. Take a deep breath and put the head back in the water until the ears are wet. Relax and let the feet float off the bottom of the pool. It is not necessary for participants to float in a horizontal position. The key is to maintain an unsupported float for 3 to 5 seconds.

Rolling Over

Mastering the *rollover* allows students to change strokes or to rest after rolling from front to back. To roll from front to back, finish the stroke by bringing an arm down to the side and looking over the same shoulder in the direction of the roll. Take a deep breath and continue swimming on the back.

To roll from back to front, look in the direction of the roll. If rolling left, reach across the chest with the right arm without lifting it out of the water. Reach to a point in front of the head and continue stroking on the front.

Changing Directions

Changing directions helps the individual return to safety. Participants should be able to swim a short distance away from the poolside and return using a wide turn. This is accomplished by looking and stroking harder in the direction of the turn. Another method of changing direction is to stop swimming, tread water, turn and face the new direction, and begin swimming back to the poolside.

Treading Water

Treading water is the deep-water support position. Swimmers who master this skill can participate in most of the deep-water activities. It is performed in a semivertical position, with the head up and out of the water. The arms perform a broad sculling motion. Sculling is a figure-eight motion of the hands, with the palms facing the bottom of the pool (see also pages 33–35). With the elbows bent and arms in front of you, move the hands toward each other in front of the chest and then away to a position wider than the shoulders. The action is similar to *smoothing sand* on the beach. The smoothing action creates downward pressure on the water to keep the person up. The legs assist by kicking downward. Use a modified bicycle kick, scissors kick, breaststroke kick, or rotary kick.

Students can practice treading water in shallow water, using only the arms for support. They should work to keep the head out of the

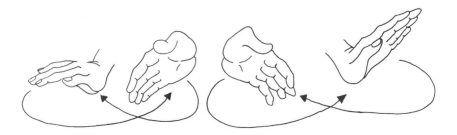

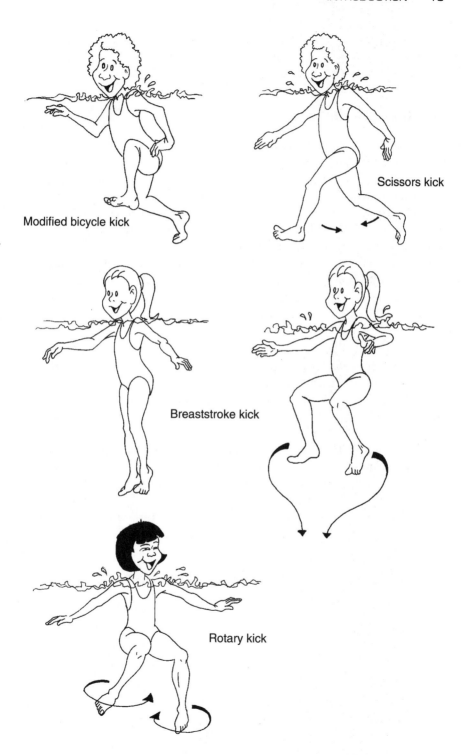

Modified bicycle kick

Scissors kick

Breaststroke kick

Rotary kick

water by using broad sculling motions and pulling the legs toward the chest. If swimmers can support themselves using only the arms in this manner, they will be successful using any of the kicks.

Using a Life Jacket

If life jackets are available, participants should know how to use them properly. Life jackets provide support for swimmers and nonswimmers alike. Life jackets should be U.S. Coast Guard approved and be in good condition. Participants should be capable of donning a life jacket on deck and in shallow water. They should be able to perform a few swimming strokes on their front or back in order to be comfortable and independent. The feet-first jump entry is recommended for entry into deep water. Have participants cross their arms over the chest, grab the life jacket, and hold it down on the chest during entry.

Reaching, Extension, and Throwing Rescues

The simplest and safest forms of rescue are ones that do not put the rescuer in jeopardy. Participants can be taught to reach, extend, or throw a device from the deck and still maintain a position of safety. When reaching with an arm, lie down flat on the deck and hold the deck securely with one hand. With the free arm reach and grab the distressed swimmer and pull her to the side. When extending a pole, stand in a stride position and lean away from the water. Extend the pole and slowly pull the swimmer to safety. When throwing, use equipment with a line attached. Stand in a stride position and throw the equipment just over the shoulder of the swimmer in distress. Slowly pull the swimmer to safety. Lean away from the water to avoid being pulled in.

Stunts and Skills

The skills in this chapter are presented to help increase independent water fun and to challenge participants to work together as partners and in groups to solve a problem. Most of the water adjustment activities and the individual stunts are lead-ups to improve readiness for a relay or other games described later in the book. Many of these skills are progressions for more advanced swimming skills. Most important, the stunts and skills in this chapter are self-paced and are presented to decrease the anxiety of competition. Many apprehensive students will not participate in a game but will gladly work on their own or with a friend to try new things.

Individual Activities

The stunts and skills in this section are organized in a progression from water adjustment skills that have no prerequisites to skills that require a greater degree of proficiency. The major objective for all these activities is to encourage independent, relaxed participation in the water.

GUTTER WALK

Objective: Water adjustment.

Description: Participants line up around the pool and hold on to the gutter. They pull themselves along the gutter all the way around the pool.

Safety: Do not allow participants to let go of the pool gutter.

Variations:

- Participants may kick on their front, back, or sides as they work their way around the gutter.
- Use a whistle to start, stop, and change the direction of movement.
- Practice bobbing while walking the gutter. To prepare for a deeper water experience, have participants try to touch the bottom with their feet during the bobbing action. The hand never releases the gutter.

TIDAL WAVE

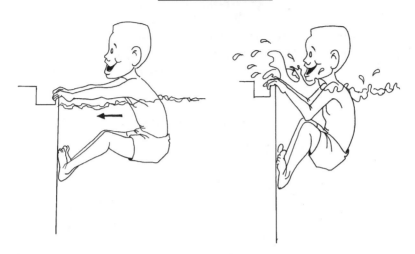

Objective: Water adjustment.

Description: Line the participants along the gutter all around the pool. Participants make a tidal wave by maintaining a grip on the gutter and alternately pushing away from and pulling their bodies toward the pool wall. If all participants do this in unison, it creates a large wave in the pool that continues to crash into them from behind.

Safety: Put better swimmers on the wall in the deeper part of the pool. Start out with a small wave. Make sure all students can hold securely to the side.

INDEPENDENT LOCOMOTION

Objective: Water adjustment.

Water Depth: Maximum, chest deep.

Description: Participants learn to perform various locomotor skills (walk, jog forward and backward, hop, skip, leap) in chest-deep water. These skills are lead-ups for the aquatic exercise activities described in chapter 4. Participants must keep the hands underwater and in front or to the side of the body to help maintain balance. Teach participants to push down on the water with both hands if they feel like they will fall forward as they travel. Use patterns such as walking in a circle, following the leader, zigzags, and circle within a circle.

Safety: Keep in mind that movement in the water creates moving water. Moving water can knock unsuspecting swimmers off their feet. This activity needs good supervision to make sure participants do not slip and go underwater unexpectedly.

OLD FAITHFUL

Objective: Water adjustment.

Prerequisite Skill: Independent locomotion.

Water Depth: Maximum, chest deep.

Description: Participants use both hands to create a giant spray of water overhead. Place one hand on top of the other. Start with hands just above the surface of the water. Forcefully pull cupped hands straight below the surface and watch the spray. Challenge the class to see how high they can spray Old Faithful.

Safety: Be sure that those who do not want to be splashed can participate without getting sprayed by others.

BLOWING A FLOATING OBJECT

Objectives: Water adjustment, breath control.

Prerequisite Skill: Independent locomotion.

Water Depth: Maximum, chest deep.

Equipment: Large corks, Ping-Pong balls, or plastic golf balls. One for each participant or pair of participants.

Description: Participants practice blowing the object across the pool as they walk. They may blow the object to a partner who blows it back.

Safety: Participants can get their mouths very close to the water to blow on the object. Tell participants to tilt their heads back before blowing so they don't inhale water.

Variation: Do as a shuttle relay.

INDEPENDENT KICKING

Objective: Forward progress using a flutter kick.

Prerequisite Skills: Independent locomotion, flutter kick while holding on to the side of the pool.

Water Depth: Maximum, chest deep.

Equipment: Kickboard or ball (size of a volleyball, soccer ball, or water polo ball) for each participant or pair.

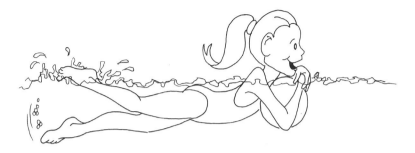

Description: Participants grasp the object and try to travel forward using a flutter kick. Be sure that they emphasize the down beat of the lower leg.

Safety: Do not allow nonswimmers to kick into deep water while using a handheld object for buoyant support. Be sure that all participants are traveling in the same direction. In the learning stages, you may need to support the kickboard for apprehensive swimmers who cannot control the board themselves. They may experience more success kicking with a ball that can be clutched tightly to the chest.

Variation: If you do not have a kickboard for all participants, use a shuttle relay format with one board per group.

HUMMING

Objectives: Water adjustment, breath control, submersion.

Water Depth: Maximum, chest deep.

Description: Participants practice humming a song, face out of the water. Then put just the nose in the water and hum to make *nose bubbles*. Challenge participants to hum with the nose and eyes in the water and finally, to hum with the entire head submerged.

Safety: It is very uncomfortable to inhale water with the nose. Be sure that all participants can hum above water before attempting nose bubbles.

Variation: Use the stunt circle (pages 2-4, 54) to encourage front floating positions while humming.

LISTENING UNDERWATER

Objectives: Water adjustment, awareness of senses.

Prerequisite Skills: Submersion, breath control.

Water Depth: Maximum, chest deep (participants may hang on to the side).

Equipment: Objects that make noise (examples: use a metal object to strike a stainless steel ladder in the pool; use a heavy chain to make a rattling noise; use a duck call, whistle, or bell; make the Old Faithful noise, which sounds like a "whomp" underwater).

Description: Participants go underwater, listen for the sound, and guess what it is.

Safety: Make sure that the objects you have chosen are safe for the pool.

JETS

Objectives: Unsupported propulsion, streamlining (finding the position of least resistance) on front.

Prerequisite Skill: Independent locomotion.

Water Depth: Maximum, chest deep.

Description: Participants practice pushing from the wall (like a jet taking off) with arms extended in front of the body. Try to glide as far as possible without putting the feet down. Then return to the side using an independent locomotion (walk, jog, hop, skip). Jets can be performed face in or face out, depending on the readiness of the participant. Performing the jet in a face-up position causes the legs to sink quickly and results in much shorter glides. Better swimmers can practice jets underwater.

Safety: Make sure that participants can get their feet back underneath them to stand up after they perform the jet.

Variation: Perform the jet with the arms extended horizontally to the side and see what happens.

FISH FLOP

Objectives: Water adjustment, unsupported forward propulsion in the prone position.

Prerequisite Skill: Independent locomotion.

Water Depth: Maximum, chest deep.

Description: Participants stand in chest-deep water. Bend the knees to push off the bottom. Push off with the legs, and at the same time reach the arms over the surface like the butterfly stroke. Try to flop, chest first, on the surface of the water so that the feet come out of the water and then splash down on the surface of the water, similar to a dolphin kick. Bend the knees and pull down with the arms to get the feet back on the bottom. Resume a standing position between each fish flop and continue across the pool.

Safety: Be sure that all participants can get back on their feet between fish flops. Everyone should travel in the same direction across the shallow part of the pool.

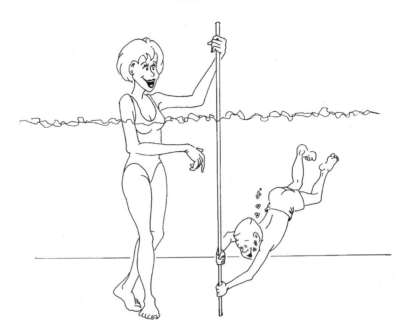

Objectives: Supported submersion, exploration of the bottom of the pool.

Prerequisite Skills: Submersion, breath control, gutter walk.

Water Depth: Minimum, chest deep.

Equipment: One reaching pole or rescue pole/shepherd's crook.

Description: Hold the rescue pole securely in a vertical position with one end on the bottom of the pool. Participants grab the pole and climb, hand over hand, down the pole to get to the bottom of the pool.

Safety: The pole should be supported by the teacher only. Do not force participants to go all the way to the bottom, but to go as far as they can. Do not allow hyperventilation.

Variation: Fire pole works in deep water to familiarize swimmers with deeper water. Hold the pole down close to the pool wall and support it from a position on deck. Do not allow more than one participant on the pole at a time. Make this more challenging by placing an object on the bottom within reach of the pole and asking participants to bring it to the surface.

OBJECT RETRIEVAL

Objectives: Independent water skills, eyes open underwater, confidence.

Prerequisite Skills: Independent locomotion, submersion, breath control.

Water Depth: Shallow to chest deep.

Equipment: Objects that do not float, one per person.

Description: Participants must reach underwater with the hands and retrieve an object off the bottom of the pool.

Safety: You may assist participants to the bottom by pressing gently on their backs as they attempt to reach for the object. Be sure the participants are aware that you will assist.

Variation: Use the fire pole to get underwater.

HUMAN CORK

Objective: Motionless front floating.

Prerequisite Skills: Submersion, breath control.

Water Depth: Maximum, chest deep.

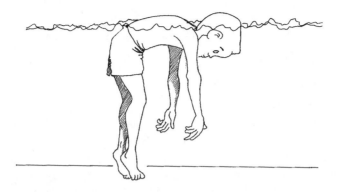

Description: There are several ways to begin this skill:

- Participants do a supported front float while holding on to the side of the pool. On a signal they let go with the hands for a count of three.
- A buddy pulls the participant in a front glide. On the signal, they try to let go for a count of three.
- Participants take a deep breath and slowly reach down their legs toward the feet. The feet should begin to float up. Challenge the participants to float like a cork a little longer each time they try it.

Safety: Be sure to pair nonswimmers with someone they can trust. Do not exceed 10 seconds of breath holding doing this skill.

SITTING ON THE BOTTOM

Objectives: Relaxed participation underwater, breath control, reinforcement of the fact that air in the lungs makes you float.

Prerequisite Skills: Submersion, breath control.

Water Depth: Chest to neck deep.

Description: Participants begin by standing in chest-deep water. Bend the knees until the shoulders are wet. Keep arms at the sides, submerge the face, and begin gently exhaling (humming) through the nose to sink down and sit on the bottom of the pool. The legs will be extended in front of the body. Participants can get to the bottom faster if they use the arms to pull the water up as they begin to go to the bottom. As soon as the head submerges, turn the palms up and push hard toward the surface of the water.

Safety: Standard precautions.

LYING ON THE BOTTOM

Objectives: Unsupported submersion, underwater exploration, control of personal buoyancy.

Prerequisite Skills: Submersion, breath control, getting to the bottom using the fire pole.

Water Depth: Chest deep.

Description: Start in a standing position with arms at the sides, palms up. Bend the knees in preparation to jump. Lean forward slightly. Jump up and kick the legs back, lifting the feet off the bottom of the pool. At the same time, push the arms up and forward to push the body to the bottom, feetfirst. Exhale through the nose and mouth to go down faster. The chest will be the last thing to touch the bottom. To come to the surface, push off the bottom with the hands.

Safety: Standard precautions.

FLIP-FLOPS

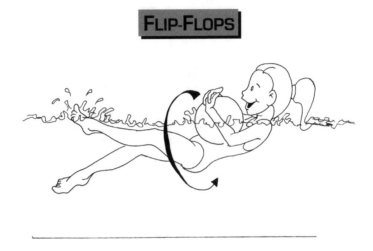

Objectives: Rolling-over skill, proficiency with flutter kick, independent propulsion.

Prerequisite Skills: Independent locomotion, flutter kick.

Water Depth: Shallow to chest deep (deeper with skilled swimmers).

Equipment: Kickboard or ball (size of a soccer ball) for each participant.

Description: Participants kick across the pool on their front or back, using a ball or board for support. Use a whistle to signal. When the whistle blows, participants flip over and continue kicking.

Safety: Do not allow nonswimmers to kick into deep water with a board or a ball.

Variations:

- Have participants put their faces in the water during front kicking. Be sure that signals are no more than 5 seconds apart.
- Use life jackets.

PORPOISE DIVES

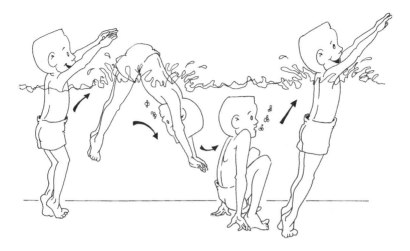

Objectives: Lead-up for headfirst entry, confidence in underwater skills.

Prerequisite Skills: Independent locomotion, submersion, breath control.

Water Depth: Chest deep.

Description: Participants pretend to be porpoises. Begin in a standing position with arms above the head. Bend the knees and push off the bottom, dive over the surface of the water, and reach for the bottom of the pool. Tuck the head between the arms during the dive. Keep the arms in front of the head until the hands touch the bottom. Push off the bottom with the hands and return to a standing position.

Safety: Be sure that all participants keep their arms over their heads throughout the dive to keep from hitting their heads on the bottom. Have all participants keep their eyes open and travel in the same direction to avoid collisions.

KICKBOARD STUNTS

Objectives: Balance, coordination, confidence, variety in stroking drills.

Prerequisite Skills: Front and back flips require submersion and ability to exhale through the nose. All other stunts can be done by swimmers or nonswimmers.

Water Depth: Maximum, chest deep.

Equipment: One kickboard (no substitute) for each participant.

Description: Begin by placing the board behind the knees and balancing on it in a sitting position. Perform various skills listed as variations or create new variations.

Safety: Be sure that all participants control the board if they slip off during a skill. The boards can rocket out of the water and hit an unsuspecting swimmer. Do not allow weak or nonswimmers to float into deep water on the kickboard.

Variations:

- Sit on the board and spin in a circle.
- Sit on the board and "row your boat." Use breaststroke pulls or crawl stroke pulls or variations of sculling.
- Perform a front or back flip. Squeeze the board behind the knees and perform the flip using the arms to pull in the direction opposite the flip.

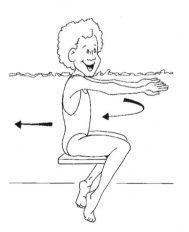

- Place the board under the body and pretend it is a surfboard. Practice front crawl, butterfly, and breaststroke arm strokes in this position. Do not kick.
- Perform a handstand on the board.
- Balance on the board in a kneeling position.
- Back float. Place the board under the feet or behind the legs at the knees.

SQUID SWIM

Objective: Understanding the action/reaction principle.

Prerequisite Skills: Independent locomotion, submersion, breath control, lying on the bottom.

Water Depth: Chest deep.

Description: Participants travel feetfirst and facedown on the bottom of the pool. Begin by lying on the bottom. Bend the elbows and bring the hands to rest on the shoulders. Keeping the hands close to the body, slowly bring the arms back to the sides. With palms facing away from the body, forcefully pull the arms (water) over the head as if to clap the hands together above the head. This is the same action the arms make when doing a feet-first surface dive. Keep the legs together and straight. Continue backwards, feetfirst, using the reverse arm pull to travel.

Safety: Do not allow participants to hyperventilate.

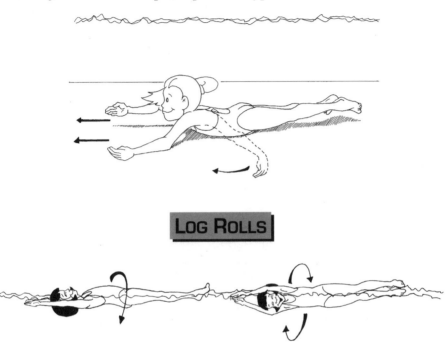

LOG ROLLS

Objectives: Swimming independence, rolling-over skill.

Prerequisite Skills: Independent locomotion, submersion, breath control, floating, human cork, jets, flip-flops.

Water Depth: Chest deep.

Description: Push off the wall like a jet and roll over, front to back in one direction as many times as possible before putting the feet on the bottom. Participants may perform this in a face in or face out position. They may use the arms and hands to roll, but some participants will discover that they can do it using only trunk flexion and extension.

Safety: Do not encourage long periods of breath holding. Participants who can do more than three or four log rolls in a row will have a tendency to get dizzy and disoriented. Do not perform this skill in deep water.

CORKSCREW SWIMS

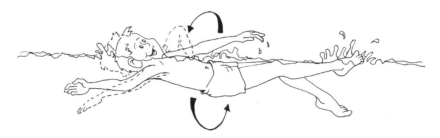

Objectives: Swimming skill, body awareness.

Prerequisite Skills: Submersion, breath control, swimming (front crawl, back crawl), flip-flops.

Water Depth: Minimum 3 feet. Deep water for better swimmers.

Description: Participants begin by swimming front crawl (face in or face out). Perform one stroke (right arm) on the front crawl and then roll over from front to back and perform a stroke (left arm) of back crawl. Continue front crawl with the right arm and back crawl with the left arm as you move across the pool. Roll in the same direction each time so that it looks like a corkscrew.

Safety: Watch for dizziness or disorientation. Have participants keep the face out, spot something at the other end of the pool, and swim toward it.

Variations:

- Combine strokes to be performed in a corkscrew. For example, do one stroke cycle of front crawl, roll to the side and do two side strokes, roll to the back and do one stroke cycle of backstroke, and continue.
- Perform two breaststrokes, roll to the side for two side strokes, then roll to the back for elementary backstroke or back crawl.

WATER GYMNASTICS

Objectives: Independent water skills, breath control, confidence, feeling of accomplishment. (These skills are much easier to learn if the participant has tried some gymnastics on a floor mat.)

Prerequisite Skills: Submersion, breath control, opening eyes underwater.

Water Depth: Chest to neck deep.

Description: Teach the following skills as you would in a land gymnastics class: handstand, walk on hands, front walkover, standing front flip, back handspring.

Safety: Spot participants or teach spotting techniques to partners. Make sure that all participants are practicing in the same direction. Keep eyes open. Because participants will be inverted (upside down) during the skills, have them blow the air out through the nose only instead of through the mouth and nose (see page 10 for a description of breath control).

Variation: To teach lead-ups for more difficult/deep-water skills, including handstands (lead-up for surface dives), begin front flips and back handsprings in the horizontal (floating) position.

SCULLING

Objectives: Control of body position using only the arms, upper body strength, treading water.

Prerequisite Skill: Floating (independent back float or glide with ears wet).

Water Depth: Any, depending on the skill of the group.

Description: Sculling is the basic skill used to tread water and to change positions, especially for synchronized swimming. Begin the progression by learning the sculling motion in a standing position in chest-deep water. Position the arms in front of the body at the surface of the water. Turn palms down and bend elbows slightly. The motion of the arms is described as a figure eight. Press the water as if smoothing sand. Palms turn in slightly as they press in toward the midline of the body

and then turn out slightly as they press out to the side. If participants are applying enough downward pressure on the water, they should be able to lift the feet off the bottom by bending the knees into the chest and maintain a suspended position by using only the arm power. Once participants have mastered this progression, they are ready to learn the other basic sculling positions.

• *STANDARD SCULL:* Begin on the back, legs extended and straight, toes pointed (this is known as a back layout position). Keep the arms extended along the sides and perform the figure eights with the hands close to the hips. Do not kick the legs. Travel headfirst by hyperextending the wrists and pointing the fingertips upward. Press back on the water during the figure eights to travel headfirst.

• *SNAIL SCULL:* Use the same position as in the standard scull. Travel feetfirst like a snail by flexing the wrists and pointing the fingers toward the bottom of the pool. Perform the fig- 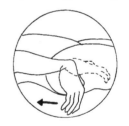 ure eights in this position and pull the water behind and underneath the body, toward the head (if you pull water one direction you will travel in the opposite direction, i.e., action and reaction). Keep the legs straight and the toes pointed and on the surface to decrease the resistance to feet-first momentum.

• *TORPEDO SCULL:* This is a more advanced sculling technique and is often difficult to learn. It is very challenging for good swimmers. Begin by using a snail scull to travel feetfirst. Keep the arms underwater. Turn palms away from the body and pull the arms forcefully to a position overhead. Continue sculling with the arms overhead. Wrists are hyperextended so that the fingertips point to the bottom of the pool. Push the water back with the palms to travel feetfirst. Feet and legs must stay at the surface to reduce resistance.

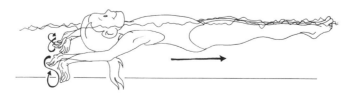

Safety: Standard precautions.

Variations:

- Use the standard scull to perform a tuck or tub position. Start in a standard scull. Draw the knees toward the chest, keeping only the shins on the surface as the knees come toward the face. The tub is a basic position for some of the deep-water gymnastics skills described next.
- Tub turn in a circle.
- Tub and extend one leg above the water like a periscope. This position is also known as a flamingo position.

DEEP-WATER GYMNASTICS

Objectives: Deep-water skills, body control using upper body strength, body awareness. (Water gymnastics is a generic term used here to denote synchronized swimming skills. Boys are more likely to try water gymnastics than synchronized swimming, which is the reason for the terminology.)

Prerequisite Skills: Submersion, breath control, swimming, shallow-water gymnastics skills (handstands, front flips from a front float position, back handsprings from a back float position), standard scull and tub positions.

Water Depth: Minimum, 6–7 feet.

Description: There are several ways to perform this activity.

• *PIKE SURFACE DIVE:* Begin in a front float position and pretend to do a handstand. Draw the arms down to the sides. At the same time, drop the head below the hips by bending at the waist. Turn the palms away from the body and pull the arms in a backward circle to a position over the head. This will help raise the legs out of the water. Reach for the bottom. The weight of the legs above the water will force the participant underwater.

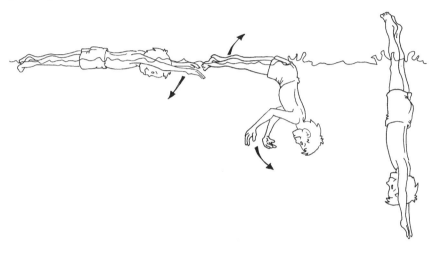

• *KIP:* Begin in a back layout position. Perform the first half of the somersault so that the toes are pointed at the sky and the participant is upside down. Extend the legs straight up and drop underwater in a vertical position.

- *FRONT SOMERSAULT:* Begin in a tub position. Tuck the chin tightly into the chest and pull the arms hard in a backward circle. Continue circling backward to return to the starting position with the face out. This skill can also be performed from a front float position. Begin as if to do a pike surface dive. Instead of reaching for the bottom, keep the head tucked toward the legs and continue pulling backward. Complete the somersault in a back float position or continue to pull around to the starting position.

- *BACK TUCK SOMERSAULT:* Begin in a back layout position. Pull slowly into a tight tub position. Pull the arms in a forward circular motion to a position behind the head. Continue pulling to return to the starting tub position and complete the somersault by extending to the back layout.

- *BACK DOLPHIN:* Begin in a back layout position. Perform as a back handspring in shallow water gymnastics. Arch the back and look toward the bottom. Continue pulling the arms in a forward circular motion to return to the back layout position. Try to keep the legs straight and the toes pointed.

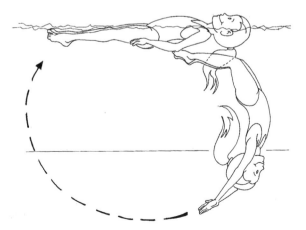

• *OYSTER:* Begin in a standard scull (back layout) position, with arms extended along the sides. Turn the palms down and pull the arms forcefully in a circular motion to a position behind the head. At the same time pike hard at the hips to get the legs out of the water. Try to close the oyster by touching the hands to the legs. Sink underwater in this position.

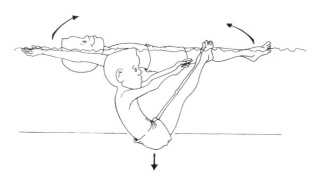

Safety: Standard precautions.

Partner Activities

Partner skills help introduce the social aspect of water play. Partner activities put the individual in a sharing position that is less threatening than in a group environment. Participants may choose a partner (friend) they trust, who will not laugh or make fun.

PARTNER TOWING

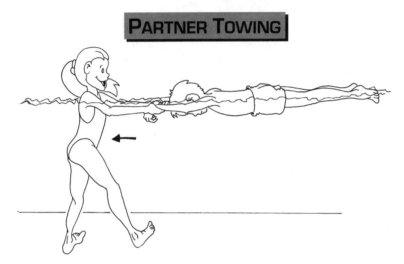

Objectives: To teach tolerance, to include nonskilled individuals in water play.

Prerequisite Skills: Mixed pairs may be swimmer/nonswimmer or able/disabled—nonswimmers need independent locomotion, swimmers must have submersion, breath control, and swimming skills.

Water Depth: Chest deep.

Description: One person walks across the pool for a predetermined distance, towing the swimmer-partner. Swimmers may be facedown, on the back, or on the side. The person towing can grab the swimmer's hands or feet to tow and may make different patterns weaving in and out or tow in a circle. Be sure the swimmer is able to come up periodically for a breath.

Safety: Participant pairs should be similar in size and strength. Make sure all pairs are working in the same direction.

Variations:

- Swimmers may partner with other swimmers.
- Use a relay format.

WHEELBARROW

Objectives: Cooperation, socialization, inclusion, stroke mechanics.

Prerequisite Skills: Mixed pairs—nonswimmers need independent locomotion, swimmers need swimming skills.

Water Depth: Maximum, chest deep.

Description: The swimmer pretends to be the wheelbarrow. He assumes a facedown front float position. The nonswimmer grabs the feet of the swimmer (the handle of the wheelbarrow) and walks or jogs pushing the wheelbarrow across the pool.

Safety: Standard precautions.

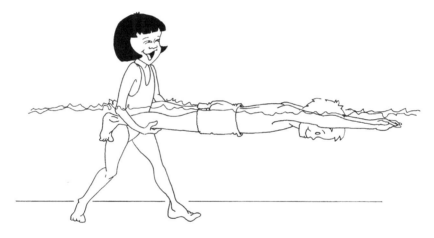

Variations:
- Swimmer may swim front crawl or breaststroke.
- Swimmer may extend the arms horizontally to the side.
- Swimmer's face may be in or out of the water. (Be sure the swimmer can come up for a breath.)
- One partner rides a kickboard while the buddy pushes him across the pool.
- Relay races: Partners change positions after the first leg of the race.

WHEELIES

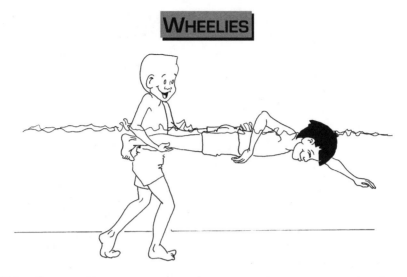

Objectives: Cooperation, socialization, inclusion, arm strength.

Prerequisite Skills: Mixed pairs—nonswimmers need independent locomotion, swimmers need swimming skills.

Water Depth: Maximum, chest deep.

Description: The nonswimmer supports the swimmer from behind, holding the legs as in the wheelbarrow. The swimmer swims the front crawl as fast as he can and tries to drag the nonswimmer forward. As the nonswimmer is being pulled forward, he releases the legs of the swimmer, who bursts forward like a wheelie.

Safety: Be sure to warm up well before trying to swim hard.

Variation: Swimmer uses the back crawl.

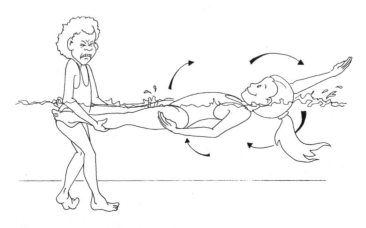

PUSH ME WAR

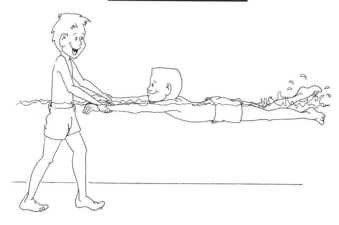

Objectives: Cooperation, socialization, inclusion, kicking strength.

Prerequisite Skills: Mixed pairs—nonswimmers need independent locomotion, swimmers need swimming skills.

Water Depth: Maximum, chest deep.

Description: Partners face each other and either interlock fingers or grasp each others' wrists. The swimmer assumes a front float position and begins kicking. The nonswimmer resists the effort and tries to push the swimmer backward. Swimmers do not have to put their faces in the water.

Safety: Standard precautions.

Variations:

• Partners who are both swimmers may both kick.

• Mixed pair may both kick if they put a kickboard between them.

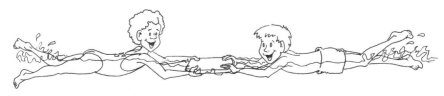

PARTNER FLIP-FLOPS

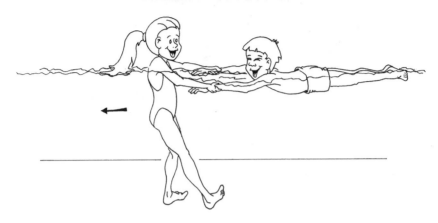

Objectives: Cooperation, socialization, inclusion, rolling-over skill.

Prerequisite Skills: Mixed pairs—swimmers and nonswimmers need independent locomotion and kicking skills.

Water Depth: Maximum, chest deep.

Description: The nonswimmer walks backward, towing the swimmer in the front float position. On the count of three, the nonswimmer flips the swimmer over onto his back. Continue across the pool doing partner flip-flops. Partners switch places, and the nonswimmer is supported by the swimmer and does the flip-flops without putting her face in the water.

Safety: Standard precautions.

BUDDY BOBS (TEETER-TOTTER)

Objectives: Breath control.

Prerequisite Skills: Independent locomotion, submersion, breath control.

Water Depth: Maximum, chest deep.

Description: Partners face each other and either hold hands or grasp each others' wrists. One partner goes underwater and exhales through mouth and nose. As he returns to the surface for another breath, the other partner goes underwater and exhales. It looks like the action of a teeter-totter.

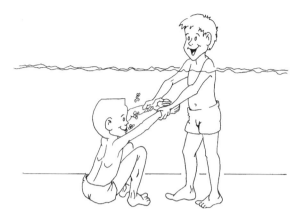

Safety: Standard precautions.

Variations:

- Both buddies jump up at the same time and try a one-quarter turn in one direction. When they land, they go underwater and blow bubbles.
- Same as previous variation, but try a one-half turn in one direction.
- One partner tows the other in a front float position. The partner being towed practices rhythmic breathing.

Objectives: Breath control, cooperation, trust in a buddy.

Prerequisite Skills: Independent locomotion, submersion, breath control, sitting or squatting on the bottom.

Water Depth: Maximum, chest deep.

Description: Partners stand, one in front of the other, facing the same direction. The partner behind places her hands on the lead partner's shoulders and prepares to jump over him. The partner in front takes a deep breath and squats down on the bottom. The partner behind leaps over, and leapfrog continues with partners taking turns.

Safety: Make sure participants have their eyes open and stay in control to keep from landing on the partner in front.

Variation: More advanced swimmers can somersault over the front partner. Place hands on the shoulders of the person in front. Push off forward and roll over the top of the partner.

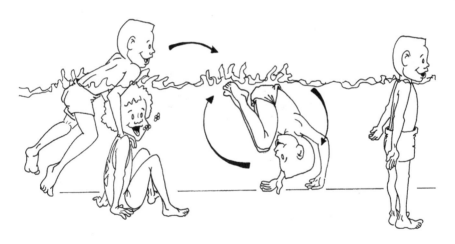

Human Croquet

Objectives: Underwater swimming, breath control, lead-up for headfirst entry.

Prerequisite Skills: Submersion, breath control, underwater swimming, porpoise dive, keeping the eyes open underwater.

Water Depth: Minimum, chest deep.

Description: One person stands with the legs in a straddle position. The partner does a porpoise dive from behind and swims underwater between the partner's legs. The two change places and continue for a predetermined distance.

Safety: Standard precautions.

PARTNER HANDSTANDS

Objectives: Cooperation with a buddy, learn to think upside down, body control.

Prerequisite Skills: Independent locomotion, submersion, breath control, handstands.

Water Depth: Maximum, chest deep.

Description: Partners face each other. One person performs a handstand. Then the other person does a handstand, and the two partners try to place the bottoms of their feet together above the water.

Safety: Partners should have a signal that means *come down*. Eyes should be open to avoid collisions. A third person can spot the pair during this stunt.

Buddy Swims

Objectives: Cooperation, strength improvement.

Prerequisite Skills: Submersion, breath control, swimming (both partners must be able to swim the same stroke).

Water Depth: Any, depending on the skill of the swimmers and the distance they need to travel.

Description: Partners decide how to hook up so that one person swims half of the stroke while the other person swims the other half. For example:

- **FRONT CRAWL:** The lead swimmer hooks his feet at the waist of the trail swimmer. The trail swimmer swims faceup and the lead swimmer swims facedown (taking a breath when needed). Both swimmers use arms. The trail swimmer also uses legs. They try to synchronize the strokes to be more efficient.

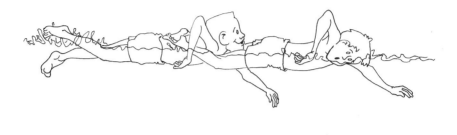

- **BACK CRAWL:** The lead swimmer hooks her feet under the armpits of the trail swimmer. The lead swimmer uses only the arms. The trail swimmer uses arms and legs. They try to synchronize the arm strokes to be more efficient.

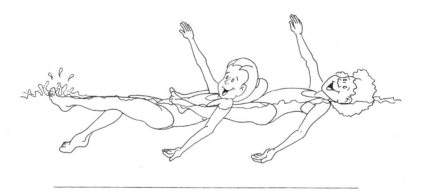

- **BREASTSTROKE:** The lead swimmer hooks her feet at the trail swimmer's waist. The lead swimmer does only the arm stroke. The trail swimmer does the whole stroke. They try to synchronize the arm strokes to be more efficient.
- **SWIMMERS LIE SIDE BY SIDE ON THEIR BACKS AND HOOK ARMS:** Swim backstroke or elementary backstroke.

• *RELAY RACE:* Swim one leg of the race, and then partners switch places to complete the race.

Safety: Standard precautions.

PLANKING

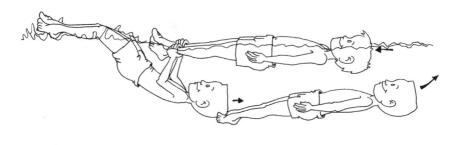

Objectives: Cooperation, sculling on the back.

Prerequisite Skills: Submersion, breath control, floating, standard scull.

Water Depth: Minimum, chest deep.

Description: Partners line up in a back layout position. The lead swimmer has his feet on or near the shoulders of the trail swimmer. The trail swimmer reaches back and grabs the lead swimmer's ankles. He then submerges and pulls the lead swimmer over the top of him in an effort to change places with the lead swimmer.

Safety: Standard precautions.

CHAIN DOLPHIN

Objectives: Deep-water skills, breath control, cooperation, body awareness.

Prerequisite Skills: Submersion, breath control, swimming, back dolphin.

Water Depth: Minimum, 7 feet.

Description: Partners line up in a back layout. The lead swimmer hooks her feet at the trail swimmer's neck. The lead swimmer arches her back to go underwater in a back dolphin. The trail swimmer helps by sculling headfirst. Both swimmers use the arms to get the chain around in the back dolphin position. When the lead swimmer surfaces, she continues to scull headfirst until the trail swimmer surfaces.

Safety: Partners should have a signal to break the chain if one is uncomfortable. Do not allow the swimmers to hyperventilate.

THREAD THE NEEDLE

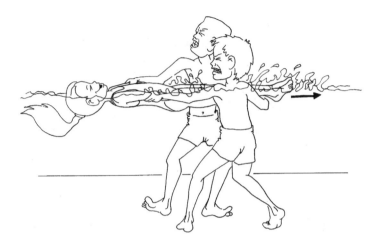

Objectives: Cooperation, body awareness.

Prerequisite Skills: Independent locomotion, submersion, breath control.

Water Depth: Maximum, chest deep.

Description: Each person needs two partners instead of one. Partners hold hands to form a small circle. One person is designated the *thread*. She tucks the knees and extends the legs across the arms of the other two partners. At the same time, the partners pull the thread through the needle (across the top of the clasped hands and to a position outside the circle).

Safety: The person designated as the *thread* may submerge and get water up her nose as she is being pulled forward. Remind participants to hum or use nose bubbles.

Group Activities

A group denotes three or more participants. However, most of the water adjustment skills are designed to be used with very large groups (20–30), with the teacher participating in the group and directing the activity.

SPLASH THE TEACHER

Objectives: Water adjustment, to get everyone wet without going underwater, to provide social interaction.

Prerequisite Skill: Independent locomotion.

Water Depth: Maximum, chest deep.

Number of Participants: Limited only by the size of the playing area.

Description: Form a circle with the teacher in the center. On the signal, everyone tries to splash the teacher to get him wet. The teacher signals stop by raising his hands into the air. Anyone who does not stop splashing becomes *It* in the center of the circle.

Safety: Standard precautions.

SKY BALL

Objectives: Water adjustment, social interaction, eye/hand coordination, balance.

Prerequisite Skill: Independent locomotion.

Water Depth: Maximum, chest deep.

Number of Participants: 8–10 per circle.

Equipment: One beach ball per circle.

Description: Form a circle. Throw the beach ball up and participants try to keep it in the air for as long as possible. Participants may hit with one or both hands. Teacher may call out *Hit only with the left hand* or *only with the right hand*. Add rules for older participants, such as no consecutive hits, only one-handed hits, or only overhead hits.

Safety: Do not allow nonswimmers to chase a loose ball into deep water.

Variation: Play with good swimmers in deep water.

CRACK THE WHIP

Objectives: Independent locomotion, body control, balance.

Prerequisite Skill: Independent locomotion.

Water Depth: Maximum, chest deep.

Number of Participants: Limited only by the size of the playing area.

Description: All participants join hands to make a line. The first person in the line leads the group around the pool, twisting and turning. Participants try to follow without letting go of hands. Participants take turns being the leader.

Safety: Good supervision. Moving water can cause swimmers to lose their footing.

Variation: If participants have submersion skills, duck under arms to make the whip more challenging.

STUNT CIRCLE

Objectives: Water adjustment, skill readiness, social interaction, cooperation, supported swimming skills.

Prerequisite Skill: Independent locomotion.

Water Depth: Maximum, chest deep.

Number of Participants: Minimum, 10 per circle; no maximum limit.

Description: Use the stunt circle setup (see page 2) to try new stunts:
- The support people turn the group in a circle.
- The supported group do leg lifts in the center of the circle.
- Try the support position in a line formation instead of a circle and pretend to do a water cancan dance (see page 97).

Safety: Organize the circle or line so that the tallest participants are in the deepest part of the play area. Do not allow the group to drift into deeper (neck-deep) water. Make sure that participants keep a wide base of support and good posture when supporting others in the circle.

Variations:
- If all participants have learned the standing front flip (see water gymnastics, pages 32–33), try grabbing hands in a large circle and doing a group front flip without letting go of hands.
- Try a double front flip in the circle.

Objectives: Water adjustment, stroke mechanics for front crawl, butterfly or breaststroke.

Prerequisite Skills: Independent locomotion, mechanics of the arm strokes.

Water Depth: Maximum, chest deep.

Number of Participants: Minimum, 4 per circle; limited only by the size of the playing area.

Description: Form a circle. Tell participants to pretend that it is a bucket full of water. Use the arm stroke (of your choice) to pull all the water out of the bucket.

Safety: Participants will travel forward when they pull. Keep the group spread out to avoid collisions.

PASS THE SPLASH

Objectives: Water adjustment, stroke mechanics.

Prerequisite Skills: Independent locomotion, mechanics of the arm strokes.

Water Depth: Maximum, chest deep.

Number of Participants: Minimum, 6 per circle; limited only by the size of the playing area.

Description: Form a circle. Turn the same shoulder to the center of the circle so each person is facing someone else's back and all are facing the same direction. Participants travel around the circle clockwise, passing the water in front of them to the person behind them. Use any stroke. This encourages the swimmer to finish all the way through the pull.

Safety: Standard precautions.

OLD MACDONALD

Objectives: Relaxation underwater, vocalizations underwater.

Prerequisite Skills: Independent locomotion, submersion, breath control.

Water Depth: Maximum, chest deep.

Number of Participants: Limited only by the size of the playing area.

Description: Form a circle. Sing "Old MacDonald Had a Farm," and go underwater to sing *ee eye, ee eye, oh*.

Safety: Standard precautions.

Variations:

- Go underwater with a partner and say something. Have the partner try to guess what you said.
- For larger groups, use a *circle within a circle* format.

WASHING MACHINE

Objectives: Water adjustment, experience the power of moving water, practice relaxing on the back.

Prerequisite Skills: Independent locomotion, submersion, breath control, floating on back.

Water Depth: Maximum, chest deep.

Number of Participants: 10–15 per circle.

Description: Form a circle. Participants hold hands and pretend to perform the actions of clothes in a washing machine:

- The circle sways side to side in unison . . . *swish, swish*.
- Add soap. The participants bob up and down making bubbles during the air exchange . . . *bubble, bubble*.
- Participants begin to run in a clockwise circle to *spin the clothes* (this creates a whirlpool of sorts).
- When the group has the water moving fast, they release hands and lie back in a back float . . . *hang the clothes out to dry*. The moving water should float the participants as if they are *blowing in the breeze*.

Safety: Don't let moving water cause swimmers to drift into deeper water.

Variation: Apprehensive swimmers can do the washing machine without submerging or doing a true back float. They can lie back, with the feet lightly touching the bottom, and still feel the power of moving water.

Over and Under

Objectives: Lead-up for unsupported floating, confidence in underwater activities, socialization.

Prerequisite Skill: Independent locomotion.

Water Depth: Maximum, chest deep.

Number of Participants: 6–8 per group.

Equipment: One ball each of graduated size (tennis ball, volleyball, beach ball) for each group.

Description: Participants form a line, standing one behind the other, facing the same direction. The lead person has a tennis ball. He passes it overhead to the next person, who passes it between the legs to the next person. The ball continues to be passed down the line, overhead, then between the legs, until it reaches the last person. The group then passes the volleyball (this time have the lead person pass it between the legs) and finally the beach ball. When they use the beach ball, they almost need to ride on top of it (float) to get it underwater, between the legs. Nonswimmers don't have to submerge to get the ball between their legs as shown above.

Safety: Standard precautions.

DOWN THE RIVER

Objectives: Improve relaxation during the back float, experience the power of moving water, learn to control body movement in moving water.

Prerequisite Skills: Independent locomotion, back float, sculling.

Water Depth: Maximum, chest deep.

Number of Participants: 10–15 per group.

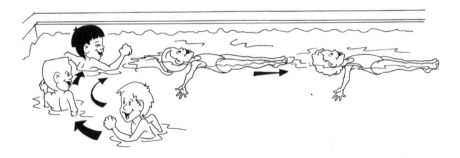

Description: Form a tight circle near a corner in the shallow end of the pool. Have participants grab hands and run around the circle as fast as they can. This creates a whirlpool of fast moving water. When they have reached peak speed, someone signals and all participants release hands and immediately assume a back floating position. The water crashing into the wall in the corner moves down along the wall, taking the participants *down the river* with it. For safety, teach participants to relax on their backs and turn to get the feet on the surface so they are headed *downstream* in moving water. Once the participants have learned how to *ride the river current,* challenge them to turn and float feetfirst downstream. They can use their sculling skills to accomplish this task.

Safety: Organize the group so that the whirlpool sends them downriver along the shallow end wall rather than toward the deep water.

Objectives: Cooperation, fun, socialization.

Prerequisite Skill: Independent locomotion.

Water Depth: Maximum, chest deep.

Number of Participants: 5 per group; number of groups limited only by the size of the playing area.

Equipment: One latex swim cap per group (have extra caps in case one breaks).

Description: The object of the stunt is to get the latex swim cap big enough to stuff one member of the team into it. Four members of the team form a small circle and hold the cap at the edges with their fingertips. They enlarge the cap by forcing it up and down underwater against the weight of the water (a latex cap gets very large). The fifth member of the team (the stuffee) is positioned just behind two members of the group with one hand on each member's shoulders. When the cap is big enough for the stuffee, she quickly jumps over the group's arms and lowers herself into the cap. This must be timed with the group pulling the cap up from underwater, or it will not work. The stuffers then pull the cap up around the neck of the stuffee and carry her to the finish line. (This is modified slightly from the *stuff it* contest played by advanced level competitive swimmers. In the competitive version the stuffee must take a breath and go completely inside the cap and then is dragged across the pool to the finish line. This makes *stuff it* a breath-holding contest, and therefore it is not a safe option.)

Safety: Standard precautions.

FLOAT PATTERNS

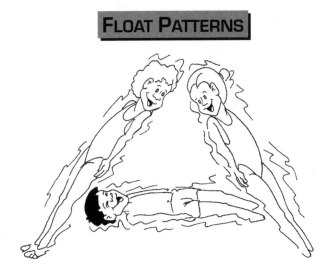

Objectives: Cooperation, problem solving.

Prerequisite Skill: Independent locomotion.

Water Depth: Maximum, neck deep.

Number of Participants: Groups of 3 or more, limited only by the size of the playing area.

Equipment: None required, but for variety use whatever is available to enhance the complexity of the float pattern.

Description: Assign a task and let the members of the group figure out how to accomplish it. For example, groups of 3 or 4 form a floating letter. Nonswimmers may be supported by swimmers or may stand on the bottom to support the floating part of the letter.

Safety: Organize the class so that each group has equal numbers of swimmers/nonswimmers. Participants should be similar in size and strength. Do not allow participants to build pyramids in shallow water. Falling into shallow water, especially headfirst, can cause serious injury.

Variation: Give participants a math question and make them form the answer with float patterns.

Games

Everyone who can move independently around the pool in shallow water can join in a variety of games. The games in this section are divided into three categories: relays, heads-up activities, and swimming activities. Most game descriptions include variations for mixed groups. Many of the individual stunts and skills presented in chapter 2 are appropriate for game and relay activities. Be sure you select the appropriate game or variation that will accommodate the skills of your group.

Relays

The relays described in this section require swimming skill. However, some of them contain variations for nonswimmers and mixed pairs. The relays can be set up using the width of the pool (using only shallow or only deep water) or using the length of the pool. A general rule is to use the length of the pool for better swimmers and the width of the pool for younger or weaker swimmers. The standard relay formation is called a shuttle. Teams are divided into equal groups, one group at each boundary. The relay proceeds with each person completing his distance (leg of the race) to the opposite boundary before the next person begins her distance. The winner of the relay is the first team whose members have all completed their leg of the race.

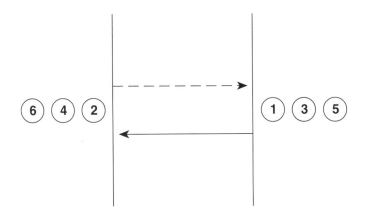

MEDLEY DASH

Objective: Determined by the skills chosen for locomotion.

Prerequisite Skill: Swimming.

Water Depth: Minimum, chest deep.

Number of Participants: Two or more equal teams of 4–6 players.

Description: Use a shuttle relay formation. Each member of the team is given a different stroke to swim across the pool (examples: front crawl, back crawl, elementary backstroke, sidestroke, breaststroke, butterfly, or stroke variation). On the signal, the first member completes the distance and tags the second person, who travels back across the pool. The relay continues until all members of the team have completed their part of the relay.

Safety: If starting from the deck, do not allow dive entries into shallow water.

Variations:

- Have all swimmers swim the same stroke.
- Assign nonswimmers skills that do not require submersion (examples: run forward or backward, hop, skip, leap).
- Use forms of corkscrew for locomotion.
- Swim with kickboard stunts.

BUDDY SWIM RELAY

Objectives: Determined by skills chosen for locomotion, socialization.

Prerequisite Skills: Submersion, breath control, swimming (both partners must be able to swim the same stroke).

Water Depth: Minimum, chest deep.

Number of Participants: Two or more teams of 4, 6, or 8 players.

Description: All members of the team are positioned on the same end of the pool. Each team member must have a buddy. Each buddy pair completes two legs of the race. One leg of the race is completed with one buddy leading, then buddies trade places and the second buddy leads the pair on the second leg of the race. When all buddy pairs have completed their section of the race they are finished. The winning team is the team who completes all legs of the race the fastest.

Safety: Standard precautions.

Variation: Can be done in shallow water using partner swims (mixed pairs) described in chapter 2 (pages 39–43).

SOCK AND SHIRT RELAY

Objective: Determined by skills chosen for locomotion.

Prerequisite Skill: Swimming.

Water Depth: Minimum, chest deep.

Number of Participants: Two or more equal teams of 4–6 players.

Equipment: One shirt and one sock per team.

Description: Divide the teams as for a shuttle relay. On the signal, the first member of the team puts on the sock and shirt and swims his leg of the race. He must remove the clothing and give it to the second person, who puts it on before completing his leg of the relay. The relay continues until all members of the team have successfully completed the distance wearing the sock and shirt.

Safety: Standard precautions.

Variations:

- Use oversized sweatshirts for advanced groups.
- Use additional clothing (two socks, a shoe, a hat, shorts). Each person must don the previous swimmer's pieces of clothing and add a piece before completing her leg of the relay. The last person to swim is fully dressed.

- Have individuals race against each other rather than race in teams. Organize the race in heats determined by the number of lanes available. Each individual has a sock and shirt. On the signal, participants put on the sock and swim across the pool. They climb out of the pool and put on the shirt and then swim back to the starting point. The winners of each heat race each other in the last heat of the race.
- Use the shuttle relay format. Each team has a dry towel or a newspaper. Each member of the team swims her leg of the relay without getting the towel or newspaper wet. The winner is the team with the fastest time and the driest towel.

BALLOON RELAY

Objective: Determined by the method chosen for locomotion.

Prerequisite Skill: Swimming.

Water Depth: Minimum, chest deep.

Number of Participants: Two or more equal teams of 4–6 players.

Equipment: One balloon per member of a team, extra balloons (start with the balloons blown up and tied).

Description: Divide the teams as for a shuttle relay. On the signal, the first person swims the balloon across the pool. He must pop the balloon before the second person in the relay begins her leg of the race. The relay continues until all members of the team have completed their leg of the race and the balloons are popped.

Safety: Participants may begin in the water or on deck. If starting from the deck, do not allow dive entries.

Variations:

- Participants must hop out of the water and sit on the balloon to pop it.
- Participants start with a deflated balloon and must blow it up and tie it before entering the pool.
- More skilled participants blow the balloon up underwater, tie it off, and then begin the race.

BALL RELAY

Objective: Lead-up for water polo.

Prerequisite Skill: Swimming front crawl with the head up.

Water Depth: Minimum, chest deep.

Number of Participants: Two or more even teams of 4–6 players.

Equipment: One ball per team, all the same size.

Description: Divide the teams as for a shuttle relay. On the signal, the first person swims the ball across the pool using the front crawl. The ball is kept moving in front of the swimmer by the action of the arm stroke as the swimmer's arm reaches forward for the next stroke (as in water polo). She gives the ball to the second team member, and the relay continues until all members of the team have completed their leg of the race.

Safety: Standard precautions.

Variations:

- Organize the teams in a single file line. Each member of the team swims the distance and shoots for a goal. Have a team member catch the ball or use chairs to mark the goal. Points are awarded for the most goals in the shortest amount of time.
- Hold the ball between the knees. Swim on the front or back. A ball that pops out must be retrieved.

- Use the shuttle relay format. Each team has a spoon with a Ping-Pong ball on it. The swimmer swims the front crawl carrying the spoon in her mouth, then hands it off to the next person in the relay.

Aqua Man Relay

Objectives: Breath control, lead-up for headfirst entry.

Prerequisite Skills: Submersion, breath control, underwater swimming, porpoise dive.

Water Depth: Maximum, chest deep.

Number of Participants: Two or more equal teams of 4–6 players.

Description: Divide the teams as for a shuttle relay. On the signal, the first person porpoise dives across the pool. He may not swim or take any walking steps between porpoise dives.

Safety: Participants must keep their eyes open to avoid collisions.

HUMAN CROQUET RELAY

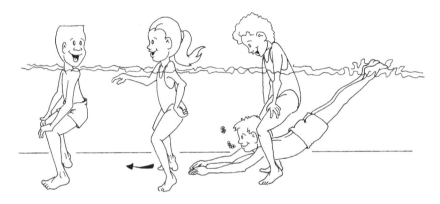

Objective: Underwater swimming.

Prerequisite Skills: Submersion, breath control, underwater swimming.

Water Depth: Maximum, chest deep.

Description: Players line up arm's length apart using a straddle stance. The player at the end of the line begins by submerging and swimming underwater between team members' legs to the head of the line. As soon as he surfaces at the head of the line, the person at the back of the line follows. This continues until the head of the line reaches the finish line.

Safety: The finish line should not be set closer than 6 feet from the pool wall. Be sure that teams are small enough to allow a swimmer to get completely to the head of the line with one breath.

Variation: Form teams of 8 (4 swimmers, 4 nonswimmers). Use a staggered line. Nonswimmers form the croquet wickets. Swimmers race back and forth through the wickets in relay format.

Heads-Up Activities

Heads-up games and relays are designed for nonswimmers and groups that have a significant number of nonswimmers in them. They can be used for water adjustment, as warm-up activities for fitness workouts, or just for fun. Many of these games have variations that require submersion and swimming skills. You can use these variations to challenge the swimmers in your group or to encourage your nonswimmers to submerge. Look carefully at the description of the variations to select the game or relay that fits the characteristics of your group.

OVER AND UNDER RELAY

Objectives: Socialization, water adjustment.

Prerequisite Skill: Independent locomotion.

Water Depth: Maximum, chest deep.

Number of Participants: Two or more equal teams.

Equipment: One ball for each team.

Description: Use a line formation. The first person in each line begins by passing the ball under the water between his legs to the person behind. The next person passes it overhead, and the ball continues down the line, overhead and underwater, until it reaches the last person in line.

Safety: Standard precautions. Note that some participants may submerge when they try to pass the ball between their legs.

Variations:

- When the ball reaches the end of the line, all participants turn around and pass the ball back to the beginning to win the race.
- When the ball reaches the end of the line, the last person must submerge and swim the ball between team members' legs to get to the front of the line. This is difficult because the ball floats. Team members find themselves playing leapfrog to help the swimmer with the ball stay underwater to get to the head of the line.
- Pass the ball over the heads of the entire line. The last person in line then swims the ball (water polo style) to the head of the line

and tosses the ball back to the back of the line. The relay continues until all team members are back in their original positions in the line.

OBJECT RETRIEVAL RACE

Objectives: Improve confidence, improve independent locomotion, social interaction.

Prerequisite Skill: Independent locomotion.

Water Depth: Maximum, chest deep.

Number of Participants: Two or more equally numbered teams.

Equipment: One plastic container for each team (suggestions: large drink cup, plastic cereal bowl). Many small floating objects (suggestions: different sizes of corks, Ping-Pong balls, plastic golf balls).

Description: Place the plastic containers around the playing area to mark boundaries. Teams remain at their boundaries until play begins. Throw all the floating objects into the pool. On the signal, team members retrieve one object at a time and return it to their team's container. The winning team is the team with the most floating objects in their container. Participants are allowed to swim or jog back to the container. Make sure that teams are equally divided with the same number of swimmers on each team. You may restrict the method of locomotion to swimming only or jogging only, depending on the skill level of the group.

Safety: Standard precautions.

Variations:

- Number the members of each team consecutively. Throw an object into the pool equidistantly between the teams. Call out a number. All members with that number jump in the water, race to the object, and try to bring it back to their team. If there are two teams, use one object. If there are three teams, use two objects, and so on. Each team member may retrieve only one object for the team. To speed up the pace of the game, throw in more objects and call out more than one number at a time.
- Divide the group into two teams. Teams line up on opposite sides of the pool. Throw as many objects into the water as there are participants in the game. Run the game relay style. On the signal, one player from each team retrieves an object and takes it back to the

team. Each player follows in succession, retrieving an object, until all players have an object. The winner is the team who can complete the task in the shortest amount of time.

- Use coins so that participants must go underwater to retrieve the object. Pennies count for one point. Each silver coin is worth its value in points for the team. Silver money is harder to see. Swimmers will have to stay underwater longer and search closer to the bottom to see the silver coins.

- Each team is given a word to spell. Participants retrieve letters from the bottom of the pool (see Appendix B) and spell a word. Points are awarded for speed and correct spelling.

PIGEON RACE

Objectives: Independent locomotion, cardiovascular fitness.

Prerequisite Skills: Independent locomotion, jump entry into chest-deep water.

Water Depth: Maximum, chest deep.

Number of Participants: Limited only by the size of the playing area.

Description: Participants line up on one side of the pool. On the signal, they race to the other side of the pool and hop out to sit on the edge. Points are awarded to the person(s) who is the first to get seated on the side of the pool. Participants continue racing back and forth between boundaries until they have covered a certain distance, crossed a predetermined number of times, a certain amount of time has elapsed, or one participant earns a certain number of total points. (If the coping or gutter system will not accommodate quick exit, select a pose or position for the "pigeons" to perform upon completion of the race.)

Safety: Arrange the class so that taller people are in deeper water. Everyone should be in or near chest-deep water. Make sure all students have enough room to jump in at the start and enough room to use the arms during the race. Check the pool deck for any sharp areas at the boundary line if participants will hop out to finish the race.

Variations:

- Select different methods of locomotion (run, bob, skip, hop, hold on to one leg and hop, swim with one arm, walk backward, side jumping jacks).

- Select more than one winner. Winners sit out one race then rejoin the game.
- Play in deep water. Swimmers will need more room to keep from running into each other. Do not use underwater swimming as an option for completing the distance of the relay.
- Use the whistle stop stunt race as a format (see page 84).
- Partner pigeon: Use the partner skills described in chapter 2 .
- Team pigeon: Divide into teams of three or four. Members of the team stop and form a letter of the alphabet or a float pattern during whistle break. All members of the team must start the race in the water.

RED LIGHT, GREEN LIGHT

Objectives: Independent locomotion, socialization.

Prerequisite Skill: Independent locomotion.

Water Depth: Maximum, chest deep.

Number of Participants: Limited only by the size of the playing area.

Description: One person is *It*. Designate one wall as the starting line. *It* stands across the pool at the finish line, facing the players. *It* turns, facing away from the players, and says *green light* to begin the game. When *Its* back is turned, all players try to make their way toward the finish line. On occasion, *It* turns to say *red light*. All players must stop where they are. If *It* catches any players still moving, those players must go back to the starting line. Glides and floats are not considered movement. The first person to cross the finish line is the winner and becomes *It* for the next game. Players may choose any method of locomotion they wish.

Safety: Standard precautions.

Variations:

- Have good swimmers play this in deep water.
- Identify a particular method of locomotion (hop, skip, run, bob).
- Have *It* face the players and go underwater for the *green light* period.

MUSICAL KICKBOARDS

Objective: Socialization.

Prerequisite Skill: Independent locomotion.

Water Depth: Maximum, chest deep.

Number of Participants: Limited by the size of the playing area and the number of kickboards available.

Equipment: One less kickboard than participants in the game, some form of music that can be stopped and started quickly.

Description: Form a circle. Place all the kickboards in the center of the circle. As the music plays, the participants walk or run around the circle in the same direction. When the music stops, all participants grab a board. The person who ends up without the board has to walk around the outside of the circle of other players in the opposite direction during the next series. Remove a board after each series until there is only one board for the last two players. Eventually, there will be more players in the outside circle than in the inside circle playing the game. Keep the players in the outside circle moving, cheering, and involved.

Safety: Remember that moving water can knock unsuspecting swimmers off their feet. Do not allow the circle to get so large that weaker swimmers drift into deep water.

Variations:

- Have good swimmers play musical kickboards in deep water.
- Use nonbuoyant objects instead of boards so that players must duck underwater to retrieve an object off the bottom of the pool when

the music stops. For safety, spread the objects out on the bottom to avoid collisions.

- Use variation number 2 in deep water.
- Have kickboards for everyone. When the music stops, players must grab a board and sit on it. The last one to sit kicks around the outside of the circle during the next music set, then rejoins the game.

FLAG TAG

Objectives: Locomotion skills, fitness.

Prerequisite Skill: Independent locomotion.

Water Depth: Maximum, chest deep.

Number of Participants: Limited only by the size of the playing area.

Equipment: Flag football belts (preferably plastic), one per participant.

Description: *It* tries to pull the flags from other participants. Anyone who has both flags pulled becomes another *It*. The last person to have both flags pulled is *It* for the next game.

Safety: Players must not climb ladders or get out of the pool to escape *It*.

Variations:

- Designate the method of locomotion (swimming, walking backward, bobbing).

- Team flag tag: Form two equal teams. One team wears the flags. The other team is *It*. Teams line up on opposite sides of the pool. On the signal, the flag team tries to reach the other boundary before all flags are pulled. The flag team receives a point for each person who makes it across the pool with at least one flag intact. Players who cross the pool with both flags intact get two points. The flag team becomes *It* for the second game. The team with the most points at the end of an even number of games is declared the winner.

FUSION TAG

Objectives: Socialization, fitness.

Prerequisite Skill: Independent locomotion.

Water Depth: Maximum, chest deep.

Number of Participants: Limited only by the size of the playing area.

Description: One person is designated as *It*. All other participants line up against one boundary, and *It* stands between them and the other boundary. On the signal, all participants run to the other boundary. *It* tags someone, and the two become *fused* into a *pair*. Each member of the pair must now try to tag someone with her free hand. When each member of the pair has tagged another participant, the four fused together split into *two pairs*. Participants who reach the boundary without getting tagged continue to run from one boundary to the other until all players have been paired off.

Safety: Standard precautions.

PINBALL TAG

Objectives: Socialization, fitness.

Prerequisite Skill: Independent locomotion.

Water Depth: Maximum, chest deep.

Number of Participants: Limited only by the size of the playing area.

Description: One person for every 10 players is designated as *It* (with 30 players, 3 people are *It*). All other participants line up on one base (boundary). *It* stands between them and the other base. (Use the sides of the pool for boundaries.) The object of the game is for participants to cross back and forth to reach the bases five times without being touched by *It*. If they are touched by *It* as they try to cross to the next base, they must return to the base from which they came and start the lap over. The first person to finish five laps (one lap equals one time across) is the winner and becomes *It* for the next game.

Safety: Standard precautions.

Variations:

- Use swimming strokes.
- Vary the method of locomotion with each game.

DARE BASE

Objectives: Socialization, fitness.

Prerequisite Skill: Independent locomotion.

Water Depth: Maximum, chest deep.

Number of Participants: Two teams, numbers limited only by the size of the playing area.

Description: This is a team tag game. The objective is to tag all players on the opposing team before everyone on your team is tagged. Each team has a designated base. Play begins with players leaving their base and daring the other team to come and tag them. A player from team A may only be tagged by a player from team B if the team B player left her base to tag that particular team A player. Players lure each other off base in hope that another member from their team will sneak off the base and tag the opponent. If a player is tagged, she must go to the opposing base. All tagged players of the same team form a line extending toward their home base and wait to be touched by a team member who sneaks over to rescue them. A player who has been rescued must go back to the home base before she can rescue a fellow player or tag an opponent.

Safety: Standard precautions.

Variation: Players cannot be tagged if they go underwater.

TUG-OF-WAR

Objectives: Socialization, cooperation.

Prerequisite Skill: Independent locomotion.

Water Depth: Maximum, chest deep.

Number of Participants: Two teams of 6–10 players.

Equipment: 3/4-inch nylon rope the length of the playing area, a bright colored heavy plastic bottle, two markers for the pool bottom (rubber bases or traffic cones [pylons]).

Description: Tie the bottle at the midpoint of the rope. Set the markers on the pool bottom, 6–10 feet apart and equidistant between the two boundaries. Use standard rules for tug-of-war. The winner is the team to pull the bottle past its marker.

Safety: Do not allow swimmers to wrap the rope around their bodies. Swimmers may want to wear cotton gloves to avoid rope burns.

Variations:

- Stronger swimmers can play tug-of-war in deep water. An official will need to stand in line with the pool markers to determine when one team has met the objective.
- Partner tug-of-war: Partners tie one leg together and then swim in opposite directions, trying to drag each other to opposing boundaries. This variation is designed for shallow, chest-deep water.

FILL A HOLE

Objective: Socialization.

Prerequisite Skill: Independent locomotion.

Water Depth: Maximum, chest deep.

Number of Participants: Minimum of 6 (12–20 per group preferred).

Description: Form a circle. Count off by fours (for larger groups, count off by fives or sixes). Each group has a designated name (ones—seals, twos—turtles, threes—whales, fours—dolphins, etc.). One person is designated as *It* and goes into the center of the circle. *It* calls out the name of one of the groups. On the signal, each member of that group changes places with another person from the same group. *It* tries to *fill a hole* left by one of the members of the group. The person who cannot find a hole in the circle becomes the new *It*.

Safety: Standard precautions.

Variations:

- To challenge stronger swimmers and improve fitness, play in deep water.
- Change the method of traveling to the new place in the circle (examples: swim a stroke, walk backward, swim underwater).

BEACH BALL VOLLEYBALL

Objectives: Socialization, eye/hand coordination.

Prerequisite Skill: Independent locomotion.

Water Depth: Maximum, chest deep.

Number of Participants: Two even numbered teams, limited only by the size of the playing area.

Equipment: Beach ball, rope or net to divide the playing area in half.

Description: Use standard volleyball rules.

Safety: Standard precautions.

Variations:

- Specify more than three hits on a side.
- Use only two-handed overhead passes.
- Place a sheet over the netted area so that teams cannot see the ball coming.
- For more advanced groups use a waterproof volleyball.

LIFE JACKET WATER POLO

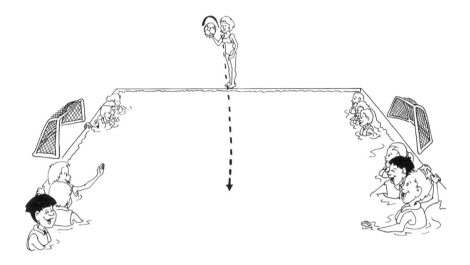

Objectives: Socialization, independent locomotion in deep water using a life jacket, cardiovascular fitness.

Prerequisite Skills: Ability to swim on front and back in deep water using a life jacket, throwing, catching.

Water Depth: Minimum, 6 feet.

Number of Participants: Two teams, numbers limited only by the size of the playing area.

Equipment: Beach ball, two goals, life jacket for each participant.

Description: Use standard water polo rules. To begin play, the referee tosses the ball up between two teams who try to retrieve it and advance it to score a goal. One point is awarded for each goal. After a goal, the ball is put in play as in the beginning of the game. Players must pass the ball with one hand to score. Goals can be scored only if attempted from behind the goal line. Adapt the rules to fit the age and skill of the group (you can write United States Water Polo, Inc., 210 S. Capitol Ave., Suite 510, Indianapolis, IN 46225, 317-237-5599 for official rules). Examples of rule adaptations include: All players may throw with both hands, players may rest on the sideline for 10 to 30 seconds, and there must be three passes before a goal can be scored.

Safety: If a standard water polo ball is used, players must wear head-gear to protect the ears from injury by a hard-thrown ball. A beach ball is a good alternative because it does not hurt if thrown hard, it takes funny spins in the air because of its size and weight, and it keeps the game challenging, interesting, and fun.

Variations:

- Eliminate life jackets.
- Nonswimmers wear life jackets, swimmers do not. A nonswimmer must make the goal.
- Swimmers play water polo across the deep end of the pool. Nonswimmers play in chest-deep water. Nonswimmers must hit the ball and pass as in volleyball, rather than throw. Ball can be hit any number of times and then may be thrown for a goal.
- If the pool slopes from shallow to deep, water polo can be played using the length of the pool. Divide the teams evenly, with the same number of swimmers and nonswimmers on each team. Keep the safety line in place. Swimmers, both offensive and defensive, may not pass the safety line to make plays in the shallow end. Nonswimmers, both offensive and defensive, carry on the game in the shallow half of the pool. Playing the length of the pool usually increases the playing area, but this method is more challenging and fun for both groups.
- Limit the number of in-water players and rotate every few minutes.
- Limit the number of in-water players, but allow other members of the team to keep the ball in play from poolside. Players must sit at the edge of the pool. They may not stand or chase the ball on deck. Any ball that goes behind a *deck player* is out-of-bounds.
- Volleyball variation: Players must hit the ball or use the overhead pass to advance it.

Swimming Activities

Swimming games are designed for participants who are very comfortable with submersion skills and can make forward progress with any of the swimming strokes. There are very few, if any, adaptations for nonswimmers. However, you may discover some of your own adaptations that you can use with mixed pairs.

FOLLOW THE LEADER

Objectives: Socialization, skill challenge, confidence.

Prerequisite Skills: Submersion, breath control, individual stunts from chapter 2.

Water Depth: Minimum, chest deep.

Number of Participants: Limited only by the size of the playing area.

Description: Designate a leader. The leader travels around the pool performing skills and stunts. Each member of the group tries the skill or stunt. Each participant takes a turn at being leader.

Safety: Standard precautions.

Variations:
- Play partner stunts follow the leader.
- Play follow the leader in deep water.

WHISTLE STOP STUNT RACE

Objectives: Stunts selected for the game, confidence, socialization.

Prerequisite Skills: Independent locomotion, submersion, breath control, individual and partner stunts described in chapter 2.

Water Depth: Minimum, chest deep.

Number of Participants: Limited only by the size of the playing area.

Description: Swimmers race a certain distance using a predetermined method of locomotion. On the whistle, participants must stop, complete a stunt (front flip, back flip, handstand, kip, log rolls, bobs, tub turn, etc.), and then complete the distance. The loser sits out one race and then joins for the next series.

Safety: Standard precautions.

Variations:

- Use partner stunts.
- Use a team of three or four. One team goes at a time. Each team forms a float pattern or letter. Teams are timed for the *whistle stop* stunt, and the winning team is the team with the fastest time.

UNDERDOG TAG

Objectives: Breath control, underwater swimming.

Prerequisite Skills: Submersion, breath control, underwater swimming.

Water Depth: Maximum, chest deep.

Number of Participants: Limited only by the size of the playing area.

Description: One person, designated as *It*, touches as many people as he can. All participants who are touched must *freeze* in a straddle stance. Participants who have not been touched by *It* may free other players by swimming under their legs.

Safety: Standard precautions.

Variations:

- *It* must tag players underwater.
- Players may avoid the tag by swimming underwater.
- Porpoise tag: All participants must travel from place to place using porpoise technique.

RAG TAG

Objectives: Improve confidence, socialization.

Prerequisite Skills: Independent locomotion, submersion.

Water Depth: All.

Number of Participants: Limited only by the size of the playing area.

Equipment: A soft rag tied into a ball or a foam ball the size of a baseball.

Description: *It* tags other participants by hitting them with the rag. Anyone hit with the rag becomes *It*.

Safety: If swimmers and nonswimmers are playing together, keep the safety line in place. All play must remain in the water. A rag thrown out of the pool should be retrieved by the teacher and thrown back to *It*.

Variation: Partner rag tag. A swimmer and nonswimmer may play as partners and pass the rag back and forth from shallow to deep.

TANGLE

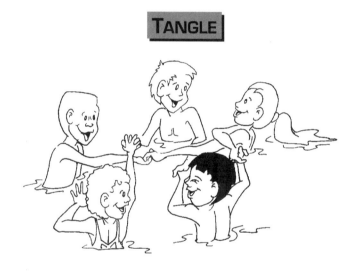

Objectives: Socialization, cooperation.

Prerequisite Skills: Independent locomotion, submersion.

Water Depth: Maximum, chest deep.

Number of Participants: Groups of 6–10.

Description: Participants form a circle. Each player joins one hand with someone across the circle and the other hand with someone near her, until everyone has joined hands. The object is to untangle the group to form a single circle without breaking grips.

Safety: One person should remain outside the tangle to help the group and make sure that players who must go underwater to untangle are not submerged for long. There should be a signal for all participants to *let go* in case someone is having trouble underwater. Do not do this activity in deep water.

Swim the Waves

Objectives: Socialization, swimming in moving water.

Prerequisite Skills: Independent locomotion, swimming.

Water Depth: Maximum, chest deep.

Number of Participants: Large groups, 20 or more per group.

Equipment: Kickboards, one per participant.

Description: Participants, each with a kickboard, form two lines, facing each other, about 10 feet apart. Participants use the broad side of the kickboard to make a gauntlet of waves by alternately pushing and pulling the board through the surface of the water. One swimmer tries to swim through the waves between the two lines. Take turns letting all swimmers challenge the waves.

Safety: Swimmers should be told to stand up if they cannot make it through the waves.

Variations:

- Let nonswimmers challenge the gauntlet by walking through it.
- Throw a heaving jug, heaving line, or ring buoy through the waves and pull a swimmer through the gauntlet.

Baseball

Objectives: Socialization, cooperation, eye/hand coordination, throwing.

Prerequisite Skills: Independent locomotion, swimming skills to play in deep water (outfielder).

Water Depth: All.

Number of Participants: Minimum, 6 (9–11 per team preferred).

Equipment: Wiffle ball and plastic bat, rubber bases or traffic cones (pylons).

Description: Use standard baseball rules. Adapt rules for age and skill of the participants. If there are swimmers and nonswimmers in the group, select teams so that each has an equal number of nonswimmers for the shallow water positions. Organize the bases in the shallow area. Deep water is the outfield.

Safety: If possible, keep the safety line in place. Swimmers can swim under it to field the ball. It will keep nonswimmers from slipping into deeper water.

Variations:

- Let participants use any method of locomotion to reach the base.
- Set the bases closer together for smaller children.
- Let participants have more than three strikes.
- Let older participants have only one pitch.
- Let participants run either direction around the bases but continue in the original direction chosen.

UNDERWATER HOCKEY

Objectives: Confidence, underwater swimming, socialization.

Prerequisite Skills: Independent locomotion, submersion, breath control, underwater swimming, porpoise dive.

Water Depth: Maximum, chest deep.

Number of Participants: Two teams, numbers limited only by the size of the playing area.

Equipment: One hockey puck, hockey sticks for each player, goals at each end of the playing area. A rubber diving ring is a good substitute for a hockey puck. Sticks can be made from wood and should be 11 inches long. Drill a hole through the handle of the stick and attach a wrist strap of some kind to keep the stick from floating away if it is released during play. Use traffic cones (pylons) to mark the goals on the bottom of the pool.

Description: Use standard hockey rules (you can write the Underwater Society of America, P.O. Box 628, Daly City, CA 94017 for official rules). One member from each team faces off over the puck to begin the game. Players must leave the puck on the bottom of the pool when they return to the surface for air.

Safety: Caution players against hyperventilation (pages 10–11). Players should wear a garden glove or an inexpensive work glove covered with solidified hot glue to protect the knuckles during play.

Variations:

- Let better players play in water up to 5 feet deep.
- Increase the playing area and allow participants to wear masks, fins, and snorkles.

BIG SPLASH CONTEST

Objective: Approach to a spring dive.

Prerequisite Skill: Swimming in deep water.

Water Depth: Minimum of 9 feet under the diving board.

Equipment: 1-meter diving board, diving scorecards.

Description: Select three people to serve as judges. Participants make three jumps from the board. They must use a feet entry. Each jump is awarded a score by the judges. Judges use a scale from 1 to 10, and they award scores according to the height and girth of the splash. The person who accumulates the most total points in three jumps is the winner. If two participants tie, they may have a *splash off*, which consists of one final attempt.

Safety: Standard diving board rules.

Variation: Throw a ball to the contestant at the height of the jump. Points are awarded only if the contestant catches the ball.

Fitness Activities

The consequences of sedentary lifestyles are evidenced in the number of deaths attributed to cardiovascular disease, high blood pressure, and the complications of obesity. A good fitness habit is a learned behavior. You can encourage fit lifestyles by including exciting fitness activities in your water classes. Fitness activities should encompass cardiorespiratory fitness, muscular strength, muscular endurance, and flexibility. The activities in this chapter emphasize the cardiorespiratory system and by design, improve muscular endurance through repetitive activity. Workouts should be supplemented with strength training and flexibility to provide a well-rounded approach to personal fitness. All workouts should begin with a slow warm-up, followed by a brief period of stretching. The aerobic activity (used to improve the cardiorespiratory system) should follow the F.I.T. principle.

- *F*requency: 3 to 5 times per week.
- *I*ntensity: 60%–85% of heart rate reserve.

• Time: a minimum of 15 minutes (within target heart rate zone). Check the heart rate at least once during the activity. Follow the aerobic workout with a cooldown period and a period of stretching. Use the following formula to figure target heart rate.

1. Subtract your age from 220.   220 – age = ___ (A)

2. Determine your resting heart rate (RHR). * RHR = ___

3. Subtract the RHR from (A) in step 1.   (A) – RHR = ___ (B)

4. Multiply (B) by 60% intensity (.60).   B × .60 = ___ (C)

5. Add RHR from step 2 to (C) from step 4 to get the lower limit of the target heart rate zone.   (C) + RHR = ___

6. Repeat steps 4 and 5 using 85% (.85) intensity to find the upper limit of the target heart rate zone.

Water Exercise

Water fitness activities are not limited to swimming. Aquatic exercise (exercise in an upright, face out position) is one of the fastest growing forms of fitness today. Its popularity stems from two important facts: Swimming skill is not required, and water offers a low impact medium for exercise, which is appropriate for many individuals with special needs. Water is supportive and resistive. It can provide an adequate overload for improvements in strength and muscular endurance as well as cardiorespiratory fitness. The underlying principles of aquatic exercise are beyond the scope of this book, but a brief overview will help you understand how to produce an overload to enhance the fitness components.

Position

Stand up straight and keep the shoulders over the hips. Leaning forward, either in place or while traveling across the pool, can increase buoyancy and cause you to float through (decreasing the effort) rather

---

*To determine a resting heart rate (RHR), sit quietly for 10 minutes. Take a pulse count for 1 full minute. Record your pulse count in step 2.

than work against the water. Bouncing and bounding from step to step is acceptable, but you should monitor the participants' heart rates to make sure you are getting the effect you want.

Speed

Speed in the water is much slower than on land. If you put the exercises to music, be sure to try them out in the water before presenting them to the class. Music between 100 and 130 beats per minute will work well for aquatic exercise. In terms of effort, the faster movements increase resistance. This equates to a greater overload on the working muscles.

Surface Area

Larger surface areas increase resistance. If an activity is performed with an open hand instead of a fist, it will require more effort. Bigger moves also increase resistance. Moving a limb through a wider range of motion takes more time and increases the water resistance on the limb. Small range-of-motion activities take less effort.

Type of Movement

Angles (movements in a straight line, back and forth) require more effort than curves (circular movements of the limbs). For examples, see water wheels (curves) and curls (angles), described later in this section. If both activities are performed at the same rate of speed, the curls require more effort.

Effort

Water provides three-dimensional resistance. Unlike land exercise, you can overload opposing muscle groups with the same exercise performed in the water. For example, you can work the biceps muscle by doing elbow flexion, palm open, and pulling the water toward the surface. You work the triceps by pulling the arm back hard to the starting position. It takes more effort and produces better results if you work the water forcefully in both directions.

Leg Works

The leg works described here are variations of jogging, knee lifts, lunges, and jumping jacks. Each one has three levels of participation: rebounding, neutral, and suspended. Rebounding refers to bouncing up and down off the toes. The feet leave the bottom of the pool and the person floats between steps. Rebounding is fun, but it takes time to get back to the bottom between steps, and that could affect the intensity. Neutral means staying at one level. The feet stay close to the bottom and the shoulders do not noticeably go up and down out of the water. Neutral activities are safer than rebounding because there is not as much impact on the joints during landing. Neutral exercise is recommended for anyone with joint problems. Suspended moves are ones in which arm power is used to keep the feet off the bottom of the pool. If you can tread water, you can do suspended leg works.

Objective: Strengthening front upper leg (quadriceps) and lower back leg (gastrocnemius).

Description: Begin as on land. Lift the knees as high as the hip. Swing the arms back and forth from the shoulder in opposition with the legs.

Variations:

- Power jog: Remain neutral and jog forward hard against the water as if to finish a race. Pump the arms hard. Hands are fisted.
- Frog jog: Jog with knees straddled to 45°.

HIGH STEPPING

Objective: Strengthening quadriceps and hip flexors.

Description: Begin with legs together. Lift the right knee to hip level. As the right foot returns to the starting position, lift the left leg (knee slightly bent) to hip level. Continue alternating a knee lift with a leg lift.

MOUNTAIN CLIMBER

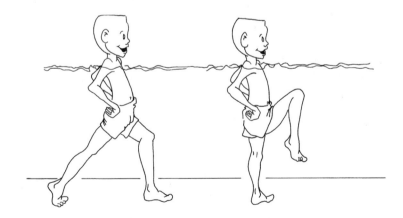

Objective: Strengthening quadriceps and hip flexors.

Description: Begin in a stride position. Bend the knee of the rear leg and bring it forward to a position hip high. Return to the stride. Repeat.

KICKERS

Objectives: Stretching and strengthening hip flexors and extensors.

Description: Begin with legs together. Lift one leg toward the surface of the water. Bend the knee slightly. Do not kick higher than hip level. Use opposing rhythm with the arms.

Variations:

- Flickers: Do small foot flicks with windshield wiper arm action (see page 105).
- Russian kickers: Squat slightly. Kick the legs to a 45° straddle.

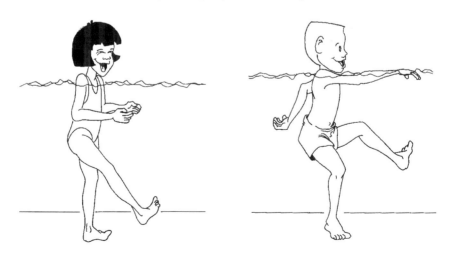

CANCANS

Objectives: Stretching and strengthening hip flexors and extensors, strengthening the gastrocnemius.

Description: Begin with legs together. Bring the right knee up in front. Touch the right foot back to the bottom of the pool, then lift the leg forward and up. Pull the leg straight back to the bottom. Alternate legs.

Variations:

- Repetitions of one leg only instead of alternating legs after each kick.
- Kick across the midline of the body, out in front of the body, and then out to 45°.

CROSS-COUNTRY SKI

Objectives: Stretching and strengthening hip flexors and extensors and the buttocks (glutei).

Description: Begin in a stride position. Switch strides. Work arms in opposition.

Variations:

- Stride wide: Same as cross-country, but straddle the legs about shoulder-width apart.
- Ski walk: Shorten the steps, pump the arms as if running, and travel forward.

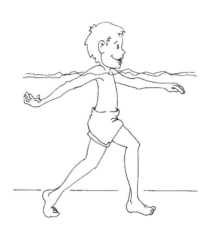

SCISSORS

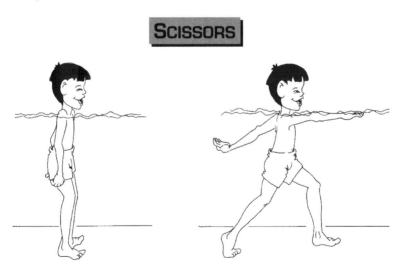

Objective: Strengthening the glutei.

Description: Begin with legs together. Lunge forward with one leg into a stride position. Return to start. Work arms in opposition.

Variation: Countdowns. Begin with 10 scissors, right leg in front. Follow with 10 scissors, left leg in front. Then count down, 9 scissors, 8 scissors, etc.

SKI JUMP

Objective: Strengthening trunk flexors.

Description: Begin with legs together. Lift both feet off the bottom by flexing the knees forward. Land to the right of center. Lift the feet again and land to the left of center. Use the arms to pull the water in opposition to the leg lifts. Looks like the action of a person parallel skiing down a mountain.

BUTT KICKERS

Objectives: Stretching and strengthening back upper leg (hamstrings) and quadriceps.

Description: Begin with legs together. With one leg, pull the heel forcefully toward the butt, keeping the knee directly under the hip. Alternate legs. (Shown with arms doing butterflies; see page 103.)

JUMP ROPE

Objectives: Stretching and strengthening quadriceps and hamstrings, strengthening the gastrocnemius.

Description: Pretend to skip a rope. Alternate a right knee lift with a left heel lift to the rear. Arms remain underwater and swing in circles to bring the rope overhead.

JUMPING JACKS

Objective: Strengthening hip adductors and abductors.

Description: Begin with legs together. Straddle legs out then bring them together. Lift the arms laterally, but keep them underwater.

Variations:

- Jack crossover: Cross the legs over the midline of the body.
- Jack shuffle: Travel sideways across the pool using the jack crossover.

Arm Works

The arm works help improve upper body strength. Arm works are much like weight lifting because the water is weighted. For safety, always assume a proper lifting stance. The back should be straight, shoulders in line with the hips. Feet should be shoulder-width apart and knees bent to submerge the shoulders. Keep the pelvic area tipped backward and the stomach muscles tight as you lift. Establish a regular pattern of breathing, inhaling on one move, exhaling on the other. Do not hold your breath.

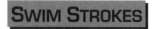

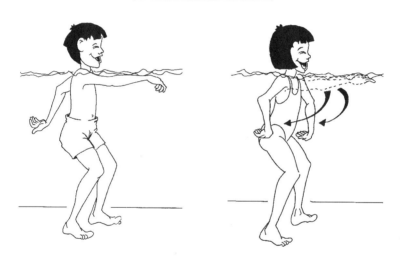

Objectives: Improve stroking, strengthening upper back (trapezius), back upper arm (triceps), midback (latissimus dorsi).

Description: Stand in a straddle position. Bend the knees to get the shoulders underwater. Practice the front crawl and breaststroke.

Variation: Use with leg works to travel forward.

BUTTERFLIES

Objectives: Stretching and strengthening chest (pectoralis) and trapezius.

Description: Extend arms horizontally to the side. Bend elbows slightly and point them to the bottom of the pool. Face palms in, thumbs up. Pull the arms together as if to clap. Pull arms back to the starting position.

CURLS

Objective: Strengthening front upper arm (biceps) and triceps.

Description: Extend arms down on the front of the legs, palms up. Pull the water up hard with the forearms. Press back hard to return to the starting position.

Variations:

- Turn palms down.
- Alternate arms.
- Use a kickboard for triceps curls.

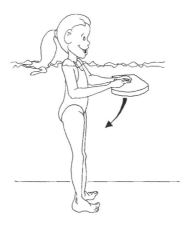

PULL DOWN/LATERAL RAISE

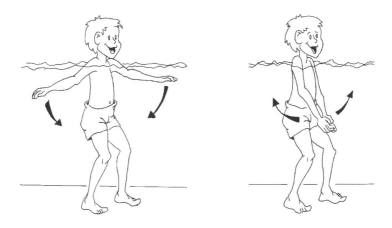

Objective: Strengthening latissimus dorsi and top of the shoulder (deltoids).

Description: Extend arms horizontally to the side, palms down. Pull arms down to the sides (pull downs) and return to the starting position (lateral raise).

Variations:

- Pull down in front of the body.
- Pull down behind the back.
- Alternate front and back pull downs.
- Pull down using a kickboard.

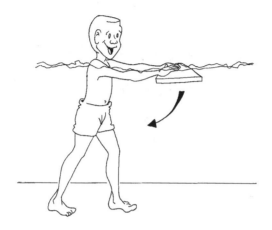

Objective: Strengthening shoulder rotator cuff muscles.

Description: Bend arms 90° at the elbow. Press elbows tightly to the sides. Face palms in, thumbs up. Sweep the forearms horizontally across the body.

Variations:

- Alternate arms.
- Use a kickboard and do single arms.

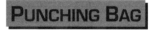

Objective: Strengthening pectoralis, triceps, and deltoids.

Description: Pretend to punch as in boxing.

KICKBOARD ROWING

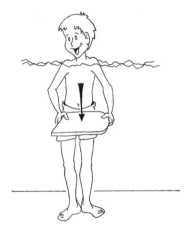

Objective: Strengthening trapezius and latissimus dorsi.

Description: Hold a kickboard with both hands in front of the body. Keep the board parallel to the surface of the water. Press the board down in front of the body. Pull up to return to starting position.

WATER WHEELS

Objective: Strengthening shoulder girdle muscles.

Description: Bend the arms in front of the chest and circle around each other similar to turning bicycle pedals with your arms.

Variation: Use a kickboard.

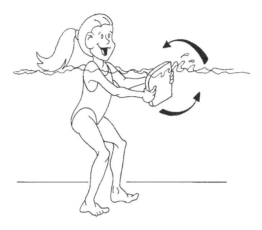

FIGURE EIGHTS

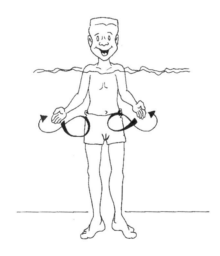

Objective: Strengthening shoulder girdle muscles, pectoralis, and triceps.

Description: Bend the arms in front of the chest and draw figure eights as if sculling.

Variation: Do figure eights to the side of the body.

Fun and Funky Choreography

The type of choreography you use with your group depends on the age of the participants. Younger children will enjoy the bunny hop and square dance moves or a follow the leader style of water exercise. Older participants enjoy choreographed exercise to more modern music. You can let the participants bring their own music and present a freestyle approach to the music, or you can count the beats to your favorite music and use the leg works and arm works or funky steps to create a choreographed workout. Remember that exercise in the water is much slower than on land. You will need to get in the water and make sure that the exercises you have chosen can be performed in the water with the beat of the music.

BUNNY HOP

Description: Use a circle or a line formation. Partners stand side by side and do a modified bunny hop around the shallow area. Leaders may do twists and turns that snake around the pool.

- Begin with the right leg. Step out to the side and back (two times).
- Step out to the side and back with the left leg (two times).
- Power jog forward four steps.
- Do flickers (page 96) in place for three counts.
- Repeat.

Variation: To go backward use a butt kicker (page 99) in the place of the power jog.

Square Dance Moves

Square dance moves can be fun and exciting in the water. Most of these moves need very little explanation. It is important to understand that moving water is very powerful. Once the water is moving around the circle in one direction, it pushes the participants in that direction. To keep the dance interesting, change direction frequently. Participants will enjoy the challenge of working against the flow of the water.

WATER SQUARE DANCE

Description:

- Form two lines, 6–10 feet apart. Partners face each other.
- Jog forward, clap hands with partner, butt kicker back. Use breast-stroke or crawl stroke arm actions to travel forward and reverse breaststroke to travel backward.
- Jog forward, clap hands with self, butt kickers back.
- Jog forward, link elbows with partner. Swing your partner right, then left.
- Jog back to the line.
- Do-si-do. Cross arms over your chest. Pass shoulders with your partner. Return to the line.
- Promenade. Participants jog to the center, meet their partner, and march down the line. One couple goes at a time. As soon as the first couple is halfway down the line, the next set of partners prom-enade. The promenade line continues until everyone has returned to the starting position. Promenade using different exercises de-scribed in the previous section (kickers, flickers, mountain climb-ers, etc.).
- Joins hands, circle right 10 steps, circle left 10 steps.
- Swing your partner right, then left.
- Return to line formation.

THE GRAND MARCH

Description:

- Each person chooses a partner, and all partners form two lines about 6 feet apart (participants stand one behind the other and face for-ward in line one and the partners form the second line).
- The dance begins with the partners at the back of the lines jogging forward between the two lines.
- As they reach the head of the line, they turn right and jog back on the outside of the line. Each successive pair jogs down the middle of the lines, and every other group turns right and the others go left.
- When they reach the back of the line the two partners on the right pair with the partners on the left and go down the middle of the lines as a group of four.

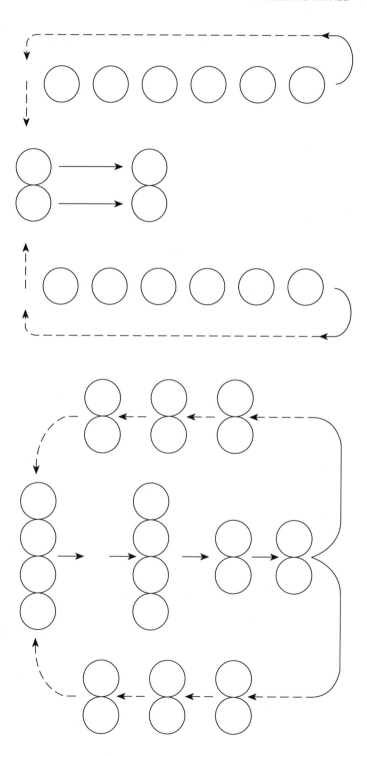

- Continue this process until there are groups of eight. The eights make a circle.
- Continue with the water square dance or make up circle or line moves of your own.

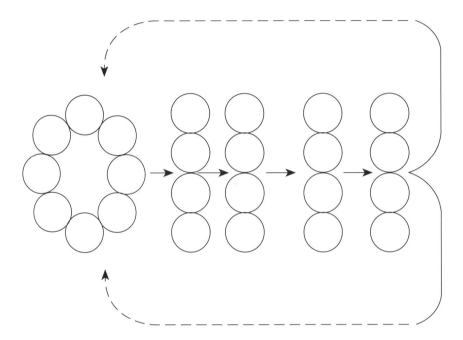

Funky Steps

Funky steps are similar to leg works, but they are exaggerated and more dancelike. Most of these steps are combinations of more than one move, and therefore there are no figures provided.

JUMP SWING

Description: Jump with both feet, lifting feet about 1 foot off the bottom. Flex arms at the elbow in front of the body. Swing arms up to the right on the first jump, then down and up to the left side on the second jump. Continue for at least 4 counts.

STEP TOUCH/JUMP SWING (8 COUNTS)

Description: Step to the side with the right foot; touch the left foot to the right foot (2 counts). Step backward with the left foot; touch the right foot to the left foot (2 counts). Jump swings (4 counts). Repeat.

STEP DRAG/SHUFFLE (8 COUNTS)

Description: Step forward with the right foot. Drag the left foot to the right foot (2 counts). Repeat, leading with the left foot (2 counts). Stop in place and shuffle the feet back and forth about 2 feet apart (4 counts). Pump arms as in running motion.

JACK SHUFFLE (4 COUNTS)

Description: Begin with a jump straddle (like a jumping jack). Step forward with the right foot and place it in front of the left. Jump straddle. Step forward with the left foot and place it in front of the right. Jump straddle. Repeat.

FUNKY CLIMBERS (32 COUNTS)

Description: Perform as the mountain climber with the right leg first (8 counts). Jump swings (8 counts). Mountain climber with the left leg (8 counts). Jump swings (8 counts).

Variation: Countdowns. Begin with eight climbers and eight jump swings. Count backward (seven, six, five, . . .) until you are doing one climber and one jump swing.

GRAPEVINE

Description: Travel sideways by stepping the right foot across and in front of the left foot. Step sideways with the left foot, then cross the right foot behind the left. Continue alternating, cross in front, cross behind.

FUNKY KNEE LIFT

Description: March in place (2 counts) lifting knees higher than usual and pumping arms. Alternate with one jumping jack (2 counts). On each funky knee lift, make a one-quarter turn to the right. When you reach starting position, perform one-quarter turns to the left.

Water Circuit

The water circuit is a method of strength training. Students can develop strength by moving the limbs at a high rate of speed. Set up the circuit by using the water exercise activities described in the previous section. You will need to

• *determine the number of stations needed.* Make an activity card and tape it to an orange traffic cone (pylon) at each station. Walk the students through and demonstrate the activity at each station. Before students begin, decide on a start and stop signal.

• *determine the amount of time or the number of repetitions to be completed at each station.* To keep the students on task you can play music with a heavy, constant beat and ask them to do the exercise to the beat. Music from 100 to 130 beats per minute will work well if you use one-half time (move to *every other* beat instead of *every* beat). If you want an endurance workout, have students exercise with 70% effort and then jog to the next station. Go around the circuit a predetermined number of times (recommended three sets). For a strength workout, do the repetitions with 95%–100% effort and then walk slowly to change stations. For example:

— Circuit time for three rotations = 30 minutes.
— Total elapsed time with warm-up and cooldown = 50 minutes.
— Warm up (10 minutes). Jogging, kickers, cross-country ski, butt kickers, jumping jacks.

Perform 30 seconds of exercise. Change stations by jogging to the new station. Perform three rotations of the circuit.

— Butterflies
— Pull downs (emphasize the pull down, relax to starting position)
— (KB) pull downs
— (KB) rowing
— Biceps curls (emphasize the pull up, relax to the start position)
— Triceps curls (emphasize the pull down, relax the biceps curl)
— (KB) triceps curls
— Lateral raise (emphasize the lift up, relax the pull down)
— Windshield wipers
— (KB) windshield wipers
— Cool down and stretch: 10 minutes.

Swimming

Swimming is an excellent form of exercise. It benefits the cardiovascular and musculoskeletal systems and maintains flexibility, especially in the shoulder joints. With a little creativity, anyone can enjoy lap swimming.

Fun Laps

The standard lap can be measured as one length (down) or two lengths (down and back), depending on your perspective. The following table shows the distance equivalents counting down and back as a lap. It also shows a yard/meter comparison.

Unless you have a small class or a very large pool (25–40 lanes), you will not have the luxury of assigning each participant a lane. Fun laps help organize the class so that continuous lap swimming can occur without traffic jams or people waiting in line for a turn. Participants may wear a life jacket during the lap swims.

1 lap = 2 lengths of the pool

Yard/Meter Conversion		
DISTANCE	METERS	YARDS
1 lap	50	50
2 laps	100	100
8 laps	400 (1/4 mile)	400
9 laps	450	450 (1/4 mile)*
16 laps	800 (1/2 mile)	800
18 laps	900	900 (1/2 mile)*
32 laps	1,600 (1 mile)**	1,600
36 laps	1,800	1,800 (1 mile)*

*1,760 yards = 1 mile
**1,609.35 meters = 1 mile

CATCH-UP SWIMS

Objectives: This is the easiest progression for continuous lap swimming because swimmers take a rest at each wall. It allows the swimmer to have the entire lane.

Description: Divide the class equally among the lanes. Within each lane, have students organize themselves according to speed, with the fastest swimmer being the leader. On a signal, send the lead swimmer off. Send each succeeding swimmer off at 5-second intervals. When the lead swimmer reaches the end wall, he waits until all swimmers in his lane have completed the length, then starts a new length. Swimmers must maintain the same order so that they all receive about the same amount of rest on the wall.

Safety: Standard precautions.

Variations:

- Have leader change strokes at each wall.
- Use kickboard lengths.
- Perform partner swims.

ZIGZAGS UP AND DOWN THE LANES

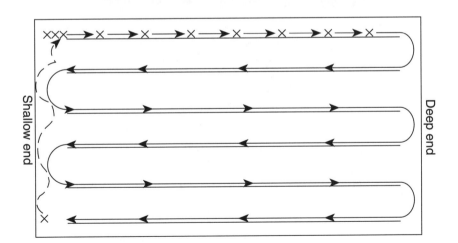

Description: This is a follow the leader swim. Organize the class with faster swimmers first. Send the first swimmer down the lane. Send the next swimmers every 10 seconds. When the lead swimmer reaches the end wall, she swims back in the next lane. After the lead swimmer has completed all laps, she gets out of the pool and walks to the start to begin the new zigzag. Swimmers may stop at each end wall to rest or let another swimmer pass. However, zigzags are more challenging and effective if done continuously.

Safety: Standard precautions.

Variations:

- Have leaders change method of stroking for each length.
- Select a new leader for each round.
- Perform partner swims.
- Have swimmers do a stunt (water gymnastics) in the middle of each length.

GUTTER LAPS

Objective: Gutter laps are for nonswimmers who want to move around the pool instead of staying in the shallow water all the time.

Description: Participants line up around the pool and hold on to the gutter. On the signal, they move the same direction around the pool by using a hand over hand stroke or a single arm stroke to move along the gutter. They should perform some method of kicking as they pull themselves along. Make this interesting by changing direction on the signal.

FOUR CORNERS

Description: Swim around the pool next to the wall. Jog across the shallow end to finish the lap.

Variations:

- Use with gutter laps. Have better swimmers swim in the direction opposite the gutter lap.
- Use different water exercises to travel across the shallow end each time.

CRISSCROSS

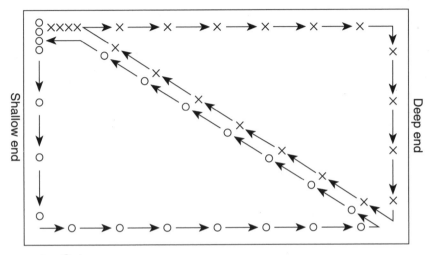

○ = Swimmers
✕ = Nonswimmers (with life jackets)

Description: This follow the leader swim is for better swimmers, but weak swimmers can use this format if they wear life jackets. The lead swimmer swims down the outside lane, across the end wall, and diagonally from corner to corner. Two groups can swim at the same time.

CIRCLES AROUND THE POOL

Description: Same as Four Corners, but keep a big circle and every-one must swim, not walk, in the shallow water. Swimmers must swim at about the same pace.

Variations:

- Swim a circle within a circle. Weaker swimmers can swim the outside circle and gutter walk every other lap or grab the side and rest.
- Have circles go in opposite directions.
- Have swimmers swim a circle in deep water and nonswimmers run or swim a circle in shallow water.
- Do figure eights.

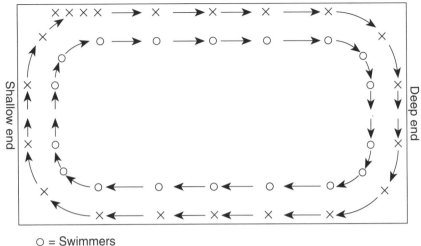

○ = Swimmers
✕ = Nonswimmers

CIRCLES IN THE LANE

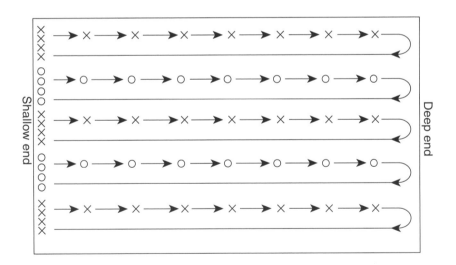

Description: This is also known as circle swimming. Most facilities encourage circle swimming to accommodate more than one swimmer per lane. Swimmers swim down on one side of the lane and back on the other. Teach students correct lap swimming etiquette. Find a lane where swimmers swim a similar speed or a similar workout. For example, swimmers who want to do stroke drills with buoys or kickboards should not be in the same lane with those who want to do continuous swims. If a swimmer needs to pass another swimmer in the same lane, the passing swimmer signals by touching the foot of the swimmer in the lead. The lead swimmer stops at the nearest wall and lets the other swimmer go in front, then gives the new lead swimmer a 5- to 10-second head start before continuing down the lane.

Fitness Challenge

The fitness challenge events can be used to pre- and posttest for fitness improvement or as the final event at the end of a fitness unit. Be sure to provide the students with fitness information and teach them how to pace themselves in each one of the challenge events. They should understand the importance of continuous effort (as opposed to all-out effort) as it relates to cardiorespiratory fitness.

SWIM ACROSS THE ENGLISH CHANNEL

Objective: This competition is for everyone, regardless of skill. It can be used as a method of conditioning the class for a special event at the end of a unit (see mini triathlon/biathlon events) or as the unit itself.

Description: Swimmers may swim any stroke in any fashion (exception: they may not use fins). They may change strokes at any time. Nonswimmers may gutter swim or water run. Measure the distance of your pool for different funny laps described in the previous section. Also measure the distance for the gutter swims and the running area. Give the students a minimum of 1 day in 3 to work toward completion of the English Channel swim. This means that every third day is devoted to continuous swim training for the fitness challenge. For cardiovascular fitness benefits, they will need a minimum of 15 minutes continuous effort toward their goal. The goal distance depends on the swimming skill. An attainable goal for good swimmers is swimming a continuous mile; for weaker swimmers, a half mile is an attainable goal. Individuals who water run should try to cover a half mile for their fitness challenge.

Place a poster board in the pool area. It should have a grid for recording distance. Each square on the grid should equal a certain distance covered (i.e., 1/4 mile, 1/2 mile, 5 laps, 10 laps, etc.). Those who cannot complete the distance represented by the square in a single day should pencil the completed distance in the square. When the swimmer has completed the total distance, the square can be colored in. For younger students use the smaller increments to improve the chances of success. (Example: Determine the average number of laps that the slowest person can complete in 15 minutes. Set the grid up in multiples of this distance.) Give awards for each method of travel.

Fitness Challenge Record Grid

Starting date _____   Ending date _____

Each square is worth 5 laps.

Felipe Mendoza																
Jessica Elder																
Latasha Johnson																
Kevin Tohei																

Variations:

- Use a local popular body of water instead of the English Channel.
- Use the Cooper 12-Minute Swimming Test (Appendix D) for posttesting.
- Use the Ball State 500-Yard Water Run Test (Appendix E) for pre- and posttesting.

MINI TRIATHLON/BIATHLON

Description: Biathlon and triathlon events are set up the same way. The triathlon event involves swimming, water running, and running on land. The biathlon event can be a water run/swim or a swim/land run. Begin by selecting an appropriate distance for the class or group. For example, swim 1/4 mile, run 100 meters in the pool, and run 400 meters on a track. The more advanced the class, the longer the distances. Measure the distance across the shallow end of the pool to determine how many trips it takes to run the distance you have selected. All participants must run in the same relative depth of water (example: chest deep) to be fair. You can run the event in 1 day or over a period of 3 days. Organize the biathlon in the same manner.

Variation: Place a time limit (10 minutes, minimum) on each event and total the number of yards/meters that each student covers in that period of time. In this way you can select the amount of time you want to spend doing the event in class. You can also select appropriate time limits for each different skill/fitness group represented in your class. For example, the Tin Man triathlon has a 10-minute limit per event, and the Iron Man triathlon has a 15-minute limit on each event. This allows you to give fitness awards in more categories. You can give awards for best in each single event and for overall winners. If you use these events in a pre-/posttest manner, you can give awards for most improved in each event and overall.

Appendix

Skills Assessment Grid

Rate each person using the following scale: + = Good / = Acceptable − = Needs improvement Individuals who can perform all skills with a + are ready for deep water games and stunts. Name	Jump-in entry, chest-deep water	Air exchange, mouth and nose	Breath holding 5 or more seconds	Float unsupported on front	Float unsupported on back	Swim front crawl 25 yards or more	Swim backstroke 25 yards or more	Roll from front to back while swimming	Jump into deep water, level off, and swim	Swim underwater for 3 or more body lengths	Tread water for more than 1 minute	Change direction while swimming on front

Equipment for Water Fun and Safety

Earplugs—Usually used to reduce the chance of ear infection. Makes it difficult for students to hear directions. Dangerous if used in depths greater than 6–8 feet underwater because water pressure forces the earplug deeper into the air space of the ear.

Fins—Designed to increase the propulsive effect of the kick. May be used by weak swimmers to experience better body position or swimming faster. Can be used as an equalizer in a game or activity situation. Can be used for fitness swimming to improve kick strength and endurance and to improve ankle flexibility.

Flotation devices—Includes inner tubes and all wearable devices that are not U.S. Coast Guard approved. Each design differs in the amount of buoyancy it provides. Most are designed to assist a learner in maintaining a good body position for learning strokes. Restrict the use to shallow water only. Inner tubes may be used in deep water for game activities by good swimmers only.

Goggles—Designed to keep water out of the eyes. Creates an air space in front of the eye, which increases visibility underwater. May decrease apprehension of facial submersion. Gives the swimmer better awareness of body position in the water. Dangerous if used when diving from a height, such as a springboard. Dangerous if used in depths of more than 3–4 feet because swimmer has no way to decrease the pressure caused by the water. Could cause damage to the soft tissues around the eyes.

Kickboard—Designed to float and used primarily for practicing kicking skills. Can be held in many different positions. Should not be used by weak or nonswimmers in deep water. If used other than for the intended purpose (as in skills described earlier in this book), be sure students can control the board from rocketing back to the surface and hitting other swimmers.

Life jacket—A personal flotation device (PFD) designed to be worn by the user. Should be U.S. Coast Guard approved. Will keep the swimmer on the surface of the water. Should fit snugly. Life jackets are the safest choice for nonswimmers who wish to venture into deep water.

Mask—Designed to cover the eyes and nose. Normally used for skin and scuba diving. Increases underwater visibility and allows the swimmer to dive deeper than with goggles because the pressure inside the mask can be equalized by exhaling into it through the nose. May be dangerous if use is unsupervised. May fill with water and slip down to cover the mouth and nose.

Nose plugs—Used to keep water out of the nose. Not recommended for learning to swim because they encourage breath holding rather than air exchange. Appropriately used for more advanced skills such as synchronized swimming skills, where the swimmer is inverted (upside down). Nose plugs increase breath-holding time because the swimmer does not have to exhale to keep water out of the nose during inverted skills.

Pull buoy—Usually made of Styrofoam. Designed to be worn between the legs (somewhere between the knees and crotch) to isolate the arms for stroke drills. Usually difficult to use with beginners, who may feel insecure when the legs float too high. Do not allow nonswimmers to use pull buoys as the only means of support in deep water.

Rescue equipment—Standard at most pools and includes aluminum reaching pole and ring buoy. If rescue equipment is not available, make your own (known as a heaving jug) using a 1/4- to 1/2-inch nylon rope (25–45 feet long) and a heavy plastic container (laundry detergent bottle works well) with the lid. Attach the rope to the handle of the bottle. Fill the bottle with 2 to 3 inches of water so it is heavy enough to throw accurately. Replace the lid tightly.

Safety line—Designed to divide shallow water (5 feet or less) from deep water. Should be standard at all pools with deep water. If one is not available at your pool, you can make one using 1/4- to 1/2-inch nylon rope (one and a half times the length you need to extend across the pool) and small heavy plastic containers (fabric softener bottles) with lids. Tie the plastic containers individually on the rope, spaced about 2 feet apart.

Weighted objects—Designed to go to the bottom. Most often used for object recovery. Examples are rubberized rings and rubberized bricks. If budgets are a problem, you can make objects using old rubber car mats. Cut out shapes (numbers, letters, etc.) to enhance learning. Rubber bases and traffic cones (pylons) also sink to the bottom and are safe for the pool. May be used to mark off a play area or design an obstacle course.

Appendix

Aquatic Equipment Resource List

AFA/Aquarobics
P.O. Box 5752
Greenville, SC 29606
803-877-8428

Aqua Products, Inc.
25 Rutgers Ave.
Cedar Grove, NJ 07009
800-221-1750

Bel-Aqua Pool Supply, Inc.
750 Main St.
New Rochelle, NY 10805
914-235-2200

Competitor Swim Products
910 Lake Rd.
P.O. Box 909
Medina, OH 44258
800-888-7946

Creative Foam Corp.
405 Industrial Dr.
Bremen, IN 46506
219-546-4238

Flaghouse, Inc.
150 N. Macquesten Parkway
Mt. Vernon, NY 10550
800-793-7900

GameTime, Inc.
150 GameTime Dr., SE
P.O. Box 121
Fort Payne, AL 35967
205-845-5610

J & B Foam Fabricators, Inc.
P.O. Box 144
Ludington, MI 49431
616-843-2448

Jayfro Corp.
976 Hartford Turnpike
P.O. Box 400
Waterford, CT 06385
800-243-0533

Adolph Kiefer & Associates
1700 Kiefer Drive
Zion, IL 60099-4093
800-323-4071

Lincoln Equipment, Inc.
2051 Commerce Ave.
Concord, CA 94520
800-223-5450

Recreation Supply Co.
P.O. Box 2757
Bismarck, ND 58502
800-437-8072

Recreonics, Inc.
4200 Schmitt Ave.
Louisville, KY 40213
502-456-5706

Sportime
1 Sportime Way
Atlanta, GA 30340
800-444-5700

Sprint/Rothhammer
   International
P.O. Box 5579
Santa Maria, CA 93456
800-235-2156

Cooper 12-Minute Swimming Test

For ages 13 to 19; distance (yards) swum in 12 minutes

Very poor	(male)	<500*
	(female)	<400
Poor	(male)	500–599
	(female)	400–499
Fair	(male)	600–699
	(female)	500–599
Good	(male)	700–799
	(female)	600–699
Excellent	(male)	>800
	(female)	>700

*< means "less than"; > means "more than."

The *swimming test* requires you to swim as far as you can in 12 minutes, using whatever stroke you prefer and resting as necessary, but trying for a maximum effort. The easiest way to take the test is in a pool with known dimensions, and it helps to have another person record the laps and time. Be sure to use a watch with a sweep second hand.

Appendix

The Ball State 500-Yard Water Run Test

This field test was designed for those involved in an aerobic water exercise program in which swimming skills are not a requirement. It can be done lengthwise in a pool of constant depth or widthwise across the shallow end of a pool of variable depth. It helps to work in pairs, with one partner on deck counting completed laps for the other. For most accurate results, runners should carve their own paths through the water and avoid drafting in the wake of another runner. Runners should use their arms to pull as they run but must maintain a vertical body position. No footwear or swimming is allowed.

Goal

Run 500 yards in the water as quickly as possible.

Directions

1. Measure pool width and calculate the number of lengths required to cover 500 yards.
2. Have a partner on deck count laps and keep the time.
3. Warm up with a couple minutes of easy jogging in the water.
4. To give runners of different heights a similar level of water resistance in a variable depth pool, select a starting point along the pool wall where the water level is at a midpoint between the runner's navel and nipple. Shorter runners start in shallower water, taller runners in deeper water.
5. Take a position in the water, note starting time, and run the necessary number of widths. Record time to the nearest second.
6. Cool down and stretch.
7. Check the following for fitness levels.

500-Yard Water Run Norms		
	Males	Females
Excellent	<6:47	<7:56
Good	6:48–7:26	7:57–8:37
Average	7:27–8:05	8:38–9:18
Poor	8:06–8:44	9:19–9:59
Very Poor	>8:45	>10:00

Norms are for people under 30 years of age and based on studies conducted in the undergraduate general studies fitness/wellness program at Ball State University.

About the Author

Terri Elder has been teaching swimming to people of all ages and skill levels since 1971. She is the aquatic coordinator and associate director of the Heskett Center for Campus Recreation at Wichita State University in Wichita, Kansas. Previously she had been a high school aquatics director and swimming coach.

Elder has also worked with the Kansas Special Olympics, where she developed a swim training program for special athletes that was adopted statewide. In 1987 she received the Special Olympics National Coach of the Year Award.

A longtime volunteer, Elder has devoted much of her time and effort to the American Red Cross. She has been a Water Safety Instructor Trainer since 1978 and has trained hundreds of instructors in 18 aquatic schools. She helped rewrite the Red Cross's national "Learn to Swim" program in 1990, contributed to its 1992 text and instructor's manual entitled *Swimming and Diving*, and served as the technical resource and on-camera host for its 1993 video, *Aqua Fitness*. She is also a coauthor of *Aquatic Fitness Everyone*.

Elder is a member of the American Alliance for Health, Physical Education, Recreation and Dance (AAHPERD) and its Aquatic Council, as well as the Aquatic Exercise Association. She is a life member of the Commodore Longfellow Society of the American Red Cross.

Elder earned her master of education degree in physical education from Emporia State University in 1985. She and her husband, Steven, and their three children, live in Newton, Kansas.